T0109544

CAST-IRON COOKWARE:

THE CARE & KEEPING HANDBOOK

Cast-Iron Cookware: The Care and Keeping Handbook
Copyright © 2017 by Appleseed Press Book Publishers LLC.

This is an officially licensed book by Cider Mill Press Book Publishers LLC.
All rights reserved under the Pan-American and International Copyright Conventions.
No part of this book may be reproduced in whole or in part, scanned, photocopied, recorded, distributed
in any printed or electronic form, or reproduced in any manner whatsoever, or by any information
storage and retrieval system now known or hereafter invented, without express written permission
of the publisher, except in the case of brief quotations embodied in critical articles and reviews.

The scanning, uploading, and distribution of this book via the Internet or via any other means
without permission of the publisher is illegal and punishable by law. Please support authors' rights,
and do not participate in or encourage piracy of copyrighted materials.

13-Digit ISBN: 978-1604337327
10-Digit ISBN: 160433732X

This book may be ordered by mail from the publisher. Please include $5.99 for postage and handling.
Please support your local bookseller first!

Books published by Cider Mill Press Book Publishers are available at special discounts
for bulk purchases in the United States by corporations, institutions, and other organizations.
For more information, please contact the publisher.

Cider Mill Press Book Publishers
"Where good books are ready for press"
PO Box 454
12 Spring Street
Kennebunkport, Maine 04046
Visit us on the Web! www.cidermillpress.com

Cover design by Mallory Grigg
Interior design and layout by: Tango Media
Typography: Avenir, Fairfield, Fenway Park, Gotham, Journal, Linotype Centennial,
Minion, Neo Retro Draw, and Influence Medium
All images are used under official license from Shutterstock.com

Acknowledgments: Many thanks to Abigail Schaefer for her expert editorial work with this book!

Printed in China
2 3 4 5 6 7 8 9 0

All recipes previously published in *The Cast-Iron Skillet*,
The Cast-Iron Baking Book, and *The Cast-Iron Pies Cookbook*.

CAST-IRON COOKWARE:

THE CARE & KEEPING HANDBOOK

DOMINIQUE DEVITO

CIDER MILL PRESS

BOOK PUBLISHERS
KENNEBUNKPORT, MAINE

CONTENTS

WHY CAST-IRON IS HERE TO STAY

There's nothing particularly attractive about a cast-iron skillet on the outside. It's all black, no shiny chrome, no flashy stainless steel, and it's heavy. And the handles get hot. And if the pan hasn't been properly cared for, it can get rusty or look grungy, which is how many of them end up at flea markets, where the dust really shows on them because they're…black.

But boy-oh-boy is there something attractive about a cast-iron skillet that's in good shape and properly cared for. In sum, it is one of the best cooking tools you can have.

AND HERE'S WHY:

Cast-iron gets hot and distributes and holds heat like no other pan, which gives you a greater range of temperatures to work with. For example, if you're sautéing onions in a stainless-steel skillet, it gets hot quickly, and it also loses its heat exponentially when it is removed from it or the heat is lowered. Sautéed onions are best when cooked slowly and evenly so they caramelize without burning. When your cast-iron skillet is good and hot and you've started the process, you can lower the heat and know that the temperature won't fall off so much that you have to play with it as you continue to cook. And that's just one example.

Cast-iron skillets can go directly from the stove to the oven, and from the oven to the table, saving a lot of additional dishes for serving and a lot of time at clean-up. Yes, the handles get hot, but they're an extension of the skillets themselves and so will never melt or fall off.

Another great thing about the cast-iron is the material itself—iron. Women, especially, tend to be diagnosed with iron deficiencies in their modern-day diets. Beneficial iron leaches into foods cooked in the cast-iron skillet. It won't compensate for iron deficiency, but it's helpful—and certainly better than the chemicals leaching from "nonstick" coatings, which have been shown to contribute to liver damage, developmental problems, cancer, and early menopause.

If you aren't sold yet, there's the durability of cast-iron. These skillets are family heirlooms; they last as long as they're maintained properly. In fact, there's something wonderful about a cast-iron skillet that's been passed down from mother to daughter, father to son, grandparent to grandchild. There are stories in your family's cast-iron skillets, and there are stories you'll be telling about yours.

THE HISTORY
OF CAST-IRON
COOKWARE

Cast-iron is the product of pouring molten iron into a mold, letting it cool, and then refining it for its purpose (whether it be a pot, a bench, a piece of equipment, etc.). The Chinese were the first to develop foundries that could manage this, and it's estimated to date back several hundred years BC. Here in the West, iron foundries are estimated to date back to the 11th century. Large cauldrons were some of the first cooking implements to come out of the foundries, and they were prized for being able to hold a lot, maintain temperatures, and sit solidly over a fire. Just as in ancient China, the process of making cast-iron pieces in the West involved pouring the hot metal into a mold made from sand and, when cast, removing the sand mold and grinding the piece to smooth its surfaces. Fast-forward to our European ancestors in the mid-19th century, where cooking was done in hearths. The cookware was adapted so that pieces could be moved or repositioned more easily, and cast-iron cauldrons were built with longer handles and legs. Dutch ovens—compact cookware closely resembling what we call Dutch ovens today—were forged to be placed directly on coals. As the oven itself evolved, the flat cast-iron skillet was created for use on an open "burner" or to be placed in the closed part of the cook stove.

AN AMERICAN REVOLUTION

Here in America, the first cast-iron foundry was established in 1619. Early settlers to the United States brought cookware with them, of course, and fashioned their hearths in the styles of what they were used to in their homelands. Cooking continued to be done in fireplaces or over open fires until modern plumbing made it possible to access water from faucets in the home. Cooks rejoiced, and running water became part of a true kitchen. Wood and coal fueled the fires that enabled cooking and heating of homes until gas companies developed ways to make ovens fueled by gas in the 1900s. It didn't take too much longer for electric ovens to come onto the scene—in the 1930s—though they didn't become really popular until the price of electricity fell, in the 1960s. Through all these developments, cast-iron remained the cookware of choice because it was still the most durable and practical.

It wasn't until after World War II—in the late 1940s/early 1950s—that stainless steel and aluminum emerged as materials for pots and pans. The factories that had been making guns and tanks had a lot of it, and the fact that these metals were lighter in weight than cast-iron and didn't rust made them highly desirable by homemakers. In quick succession all manner of pots and pans were formed with these metals, and a nonstick coating was developed to make their care even easier. Teflon was approved by the US Food and Drug

Administration in 1960, and its popularity took off, pushing cast-iron to the back of the cabinet.

THE RESURGENCE OF ITS USE AND POPULARITY

It seems cooks started dragging the cast-iron skillets out from the backs of their pantries in earnest again by the late 2000s. The trend was confirmed when the *LA Times* published an article in November 2012 declaring, "Cast-iron enjoys a comeback among cooks." The author, Noelle Carter, attributed part of the resurgence to the fact that the company making the cookware—Lodge Manufacturing—had introduced pre-seasoned cast-iron. According to Lodge, this was an industry first that has now become an industry standard, as it eliminates having to continually season the cookware.

For me, personally, I have skillets and Dutch ovens that I've inherited, and some that I've purchased. Being careful to care for the cookware (as detailed in the next chapter), I have found it to always live up to my expectations. My cast-iron cookware heats beautifully and without smoking even without the addition of oil or fat in the skillet; the things I cook in it come out without sticking to the surface; it's a joy to be able to start something on the stove and then finish it in the oven; they seem to get better and better with use (which is not

true of Teflon-coated pans); and maybe best of all, my kids have taken to using them and discovering their simplicity and practicality (though I have to remind them about not using soap to clean them).

With cast-iron cookware, you, too, will quickly learn that the variety of dishes you may be able to prepare is merely limited by your imagination!

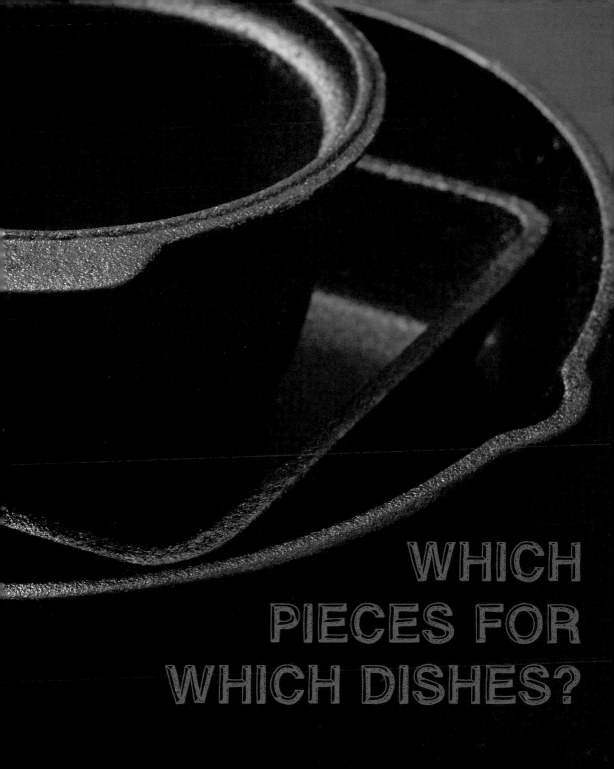

WHICH
PIECES FOR
WHICH DISHES?

Now that cast-iron is popular again, you can find skillets and other pieces in a range of sizes. If you do an online search for cast-iron cookware, you'll find two names that come up a lot: Lodge and Williams-Sonoma. Lodge is a manufacturer (see sidebar), and you can buy pieces directly from them, or from retailers that sell their products. A manufacturer of enamel-coated cast-iron is the French company, Le Creuset. Williams-Sonoma sells it in many colors and sizes, and it's beautiful (if heavy). As with most things, you'll get what you pay for with your cast-iron, too. A simple skillet may look pricey compared to stainless steel or Teflon, but considering you'll be using it almost daily for decades and it'll just be getting better, it's a necessary investment. Lodge and Le Creuset are manufacturers you can completely trust.

Lodge makes skillets ranging from 3.5 inches in diameter up to 13.25 inches in diameter. They also make deep skillets, griddles (and covers), Dutch ovens, and specialized bakeware like cornstick pans and mini cake pans.

You are welcome to experiment with any of the sizes, but for recipes in this book, I used a 12-inch skillet, or a 7-quart Dutch oven (for bread recipes pages 92-115 only).

Seasoning Vs. Pre-Seasoned

The concept of seasoning a cast-iron skillet or other piece of cookware is to protect it from rusting and to aid in proper cooking. Part of the reason cast-iron fell out of favor with home cooks was that keeping the cookware properly seasoned was an essential chore. When Lodge introduced pre-seasoned cast-iron in the early 2000s, keeping the cookware seasoned became a whole lot easier. The cookware now has a nice sheen and surface that ensures great results right from the start. The seasoning process Lodge does to its cookware uses vegetable oil, just as cooks were instructed to do when seasoning their unseasoned cookware for the first time. And it doesn't hurt a pre-seasoned piece to get "re-seasoned" using the process outlined in the next section.

The important thing is the maintenance of the cookware. When it is washed (without soap), dried thoroughly (including the bottom, sides, and handles), and rubbed with enough vegetable oil to give it a smooth shine without appearing oily, then the cookware is ready for its next assignment.

Lodge Manufacturing

The history of the oldest US manufacturer of cast-iron cookware is impressive. It all started when Joseph Lodge settled with his family in ███ Pittsburgh, Tennessee in the late 1800s. Lodge opened the Blacklock Foundry there in 1896, named after a minister who was a friend. A fire struck in 1910, and the foundry was rebuilt just blocks from its original location. It was renamed the Lodge Manufacturing Company.

Next came two World Wars and the Great Depression. The factory managed to survive by casting decorative pieces for a richer clientele until it could get back to focusing on cookware. The family persisted in modernizing its facility. Two neighboring foundries closed by the 1940s. Business wasn't booming for Lodge after that, either, but it survived because of the quality and durability of the product and the efficiency with which its products were—and continue to be—made. The breakthrough for the company was the introduction of pre-seasoned pieces, which took the confusion out of prepping the cookware for use. Another reason cast-iron made a comeback is because the seasoning is non-toxic (vegetable oil)—which became important when Teflon's role in health problems started to be questioned. And of course, the cookware will have a very long lifetime.

Today, the factory is thriving in the otherwise sleepy town of South Pittsburg, Tennessee, whose population hovers at about 3,300. Nearly everyone knows someone who works for Lodge. A 2014 report in Bloomberg Business said, "According to the Cookware Manufacturers Association, shipments of cast-iron and similar enameled products in the U.S. have increased more than 225 percent since 2003—rising from $35 million to more than $114 million—while shipments of cookware in general increased by just a third." That's good news for Lodge, which celebrated its 120th anniversary last year. The challenge now becomes how to maintain the popularity of something, that, with proper care, you don't really need to buy another of for about 100 years. Last but not least, if you're ever in South Pittsburg, you can visit the Lodge Factory Store, where over 2000 products are sold, and if you go in late April, you might catch the National Cornbread Festival (www.nationalcornbread.com). Thank you, Lodge!

THE CARE & KEEPING OF YOUR CAST-IRON

We cooks have so many options when it comes to preparing foods: ovens, stoves, microwaves, grills, stainless steel, crockery, electric slow cookers, and woks. Among all these choices, a very old cooking tool—cast-iron is experiencing a renaissance of sorts in the modern kitchen. When you season and prep cast-iron and start using it to make the delectable selection of recipes in this cookbook, you'll soon discover why it has stood the test of time—and is redefining the modern family's practices.

You may already be familiar with a cast-iron skillet. It's the plain, black, one-piece pan that always seemed to be at the back of the stack of fry pans in the cupboard. If you can remember where you saw that old pan, by all means, go get it. Acquiring a piece of cast-iron cookware from someone in your family is a way of keeping history alive. You'll be carrying on a tradition of cooking and serving foods that has been passed through generations. If, on the other hand, you're new to using cast-iron and you are the one to acquire it in your family, you can look forward to sharing its results with your family and to someday passing it on to your children or grandchildren.

Besides being an amazing piece of cookware, cast-iron does, indeed, last a lifetime (or more)—so long as it's properly cared for. It's simple enough to do, but it's important to do it properly, not only before you use a pan for the first time but before and after every use. Here's how it is done.

SEASONING A NEW SKILLET

When I went shopping for a new cast-iron skillet, I came upon Lodge pans—a company that has been making cast-iron skillets since the late 1800s. They brand themselves as "America's Original Cookware." Since nothing stands completely still, they have recently developed a method to season their cookware so that it will last as it always has but with minimal (consistent) care. That's a good thing! What they do is coat the pan with vegetable oil and bake it in at very high heat, which is just what you need to do to an unseasoned pan. With a new Lodge seasoned piece, you can be cooking from it almost immediately.

Wash with hot, soapy water.

Rinse and dry thoroughly.

If there's any rust on the pan, sand it lightly with fine-grained sandpaper. Apply Coca-Cola to the rust spots and leave on for 10 to 15 minutes. Wash again with soapy water, rinse, dry and put the skillet on a burner over low heat to dry any excess moisture.

If there's no rust, after drying the cookware all over, apply a light layer of cooking oil (vegetable oil, NOT olive oil, butter, or margarine!) all over the pan with a paper towel, rubbing even the handle. The pan should have a light sheen to it.

Place the skillet upside down on the middle rack of the oven and preheat the oven to 400 degrees (with the pan inside). Put a piece of foil or a baking dish on the lower rack to catch any drips of oil. Let the pan cook in the oven for about 2 hours.

Turn the oven off and let the pan cool (upside down) in the oven.

Take it out, wipe it down with a clean paper towel, and it's good to go.

If your pan has taken on a slightly brown color, you can repeat the process, which will further season the pan and darken its color, improving its appearance. This will also happen over time.

CARING FOR YOUR CAST-IRON

Rule #1: Never wash your seasoned pan with soapy water!

Rule #2: Never put a cast-iron pan in the dishwasher!

Why? Soap breaks down the protective seasoning, and you have to re-season the pan all over again. Leaving any kind of water on the pan will lead to rusting, which will demand re-seasoning from the beginning. It seems counter-intuitive, especially when you're used to thinking "it's not clean unless it's been washed in (really) hot, soapy water," but it's actually a great thing about cast-iron.

After you've cooked in your skillet, clean it with hot water (no soap) and a plastic, rough-surfaced scrub brush. Dry the cookware completely (all over) after washing. Put a teaspoon of vegetable oil in the pan and, with a paper towel, rub it in all over the pan until it has a nice sheen.

Rule #3: Never use steel wool!

Cast-iron is a softer material compared to steel. Any particularly abrasive sponge on your cast-iron has the potential to scratch the surface enamel or otherwise strip your pan's seasoning.

If there's a mess that water and sponge cannot handle, you can create a scrubbing paste by adding coarse kosher salt to your hot water before using your scrub brush or sponge to loosen the food off the pan. Stubborn residues may also be loosened from your cast-iron by soaking very briefly in water but do not leave your pan submerged in water. You can also simmer the mess over medium-low heat to aid in loosening up more extreme grime.

Never clean your pan by burning it in a fire! The rapid overheating of the metal can cause warps, cracks, red patchy scales, or brittleness that compromises the structure of your pan, and can sometimes make it no longer able to hold its protective seasoning.

Again, once scrubbed of leftovers, dry your cast-iron extremely well and rejuvenate the lovely sheen by rubbing in the vegetable oil, wiping excess off with a clean paper towel.

Rule #4: Store your cast-iron in a dry place!

Good air circulation and a moisture-free environment will ensure your pan stays rust-free and clean until the next time you wish to use it. If you need to stack it with other pans in your pantry or cupboard, put paper towels between the cookware to prevent scratches or other damage. Dutch ovens should be stored with their lids off, so that no moisture is trapped within.

Storing cast-iron within your oven is also a popular option, so that it is nearby and ready for use whenever you're cooking. Just be sure to remove any pans before pre-heating your oven (I couldn't tell you how many times I've discovered the pan I needed after the oven was warm)! Or you can leave it on your stovetop if you find you can't seem to cook a meal without it. An overhead rack is equally a good option, but if you have multiple cast-iron skillets, simply make sure that your cookware rack

CAST-IRON COOKWARE: THE CARE & KEEPING HANDBOOK

is well bolted to your ceiling and is prepared to handle the weight. Both of these options display your rustic, heirloom cookware proudly, and make a beautiful aesthetic statement for your kitchen.

GIVE IT A LOT OF LOVE

The best thing to do with your cast-iron skillet is USE IT! When you start using it for all the different things it can do (as evidenced by the diversity of recipes in this book), you'll probably find that the skillet lives on your stovetop, waiting for its next assignment. The more you use it, the better it gets. Nothing will stick to its surface. You can go from the frying pan to the fire, as it were, starting a dish on the stove and finishing it in the oven. You can cook your skillet to a very high heat (or put it in the campfire), and it'll cook up the food you put in it beautifully (so long as you keep an eye on it).

In short, with regular use, the cast-iron skillet truly is a pan that will just keep cooking and cooking, getting better and better with age and use. Just like you and me!

The thing I've learned about cast-iron skillets is that, once you start using them regularly, they truly become your go-to cooking instruments. They're so versatile and so easy to use. They conduct heat beautifully, and the fact that they can go from stovetop to oven is a real bonus. Here's why: Flavor. And, yes, the overall look of the meal served in the cast-iron. There's something very elemental about it.

ANTIQUING &
RESTORATION

For cast-iron pans and Dutch ovens not handed down in the family, their next destination is probably the local antique house or flea market, awaiting a new owner to come and give these pans the love they need and deserve. The thought of a second-hand pan may deter some individuals, however. Where has it been? How do you know it isn't damaged? Certainly there's no recovery for that rusted, cruddy mess.

A little elbow grease can save any cast-iron that still has an intact structure without cracks or dings; any pan can be made up to look nearly—if not just as good as—a pan bought new from a modern manufacturer. It's very little trouble if you know the right techniques, and you can build yourself a well-rounded cast-iron collection for a thrifty fraction of the price of new pans!

FINDING A GOOD CAST-IRON

There are a few pointers to keep in mind. First thing to look out for is rust of course, but take note of the color. The common misconception is that a different color of rust means a different metal composition of the pan, when the color actually hints to how long the rust has corroded the pan. A light, dusty orange rust is only surface level and easily manageable. Be cautious with pans that have flaking, red-brown rust. That is a sign of corrosion that's been around a while, possibly pitting the pan (a term for the divots of metal rust has eaten away).

Other discoloration to be cautious about is a patchy, sometimes scaly, dull red discoloration to the metal itself, as that is typically an indication that the pan was previously cleaned in fire. This means the metal is compromised, as overheating has changed the molecular structure itself. The pan is more brittle and pliable than a normal pan, and potentially won't even hold a protective seasoning anymore.

Next, you will want to access the structure of the pan to see if there are any hairline cracks. One test is to tap it with a dull instrument, such as a wooden spoon. A pan with a good, intact core should produce a lasting note, much like a bell, whereas a cracked one will have a dull and short-lived note. However, there are some shortcomings to this technique. Heavier pans won't produce as noticeable a din as a thinner, lighter pan, and any obscuring buildup on the surface will also suppress vibrations. Be subjective with this test, and don't prioritize this over a visual inspection.

Another defect to look out for is any warping to the pan. This is a sign of previous thermal shock, or improper rapid heating and cooling. Some warps can be seen with the eye or sensed with touch, while others are discerned by whether or not the pan wobbles or rocks when on a level surface. Any upward warping (causing a concave bottom) will allow the pan to sit flat, but will always pool any liquid or send a round item like a marble to the outer edge of the pan's interior. Be sure to account for any build-up of grime on the pan in your test, as cleaning may reveal a wobble or bump

where there wasn't one before. If the defects are only minor, they don't have to rule out a pan completely. Keep in mind what you want to use the pan for, as well as your house's stove: only glass-top electric burners require as flat a contact as you can find, but otherwise using a slightly warped pan on a gas range, electric coils, or in the oven will still heat the pan evenly and won't affect your cooking.

Be cautious about China-made cast-iron. These are typically knock-off reproductions that don't have the same level of casting quality as American or European-made cast-iron. Much of the time, Chinese pans are made with recycled iron or are not even pure iron to save on production costs, containing mixed metal that won't heat evenly as cast-iron pans are renowned for. There will typically be flaws in the casting and the finishing will be lacking

the polished-smooth surface when visually compared to a genuine article.

Only get pans you can look at and pick up yourself if you're shopping online on sites such as Craigslist or Ebay! You never want to buy an antique such as this without the visual inspection and experience of touching what you're going to buy, but you'll also be saving money by driving to the seller and getting the product yourself. Sellers may not always be aware cast-iron can dent and crack if not packaged correctly, plus cast-iron is heavy! You don't want to overpay with shipping charges when you don't have to.

And of course, ask the seller questions about the pan's previous owner. Find out where the pan came from and how long the previous owner had it. The history of cast-iron, even if it's not from a family member of your own, is part of their great charm and nostalgia.

CAST-IRON COOKWARE: THE CARE & KEEPING HANDBOOK

DIAMONDS IN
THE ROUGH

So how do you know how old a pan is, or which manufacturer made it? There's far more many nuances than I may be able to explain here, but I can run through a few tips and tricks for finding a pan of noteworthy heritage.

Vintage is a term used by collectors for items that are more than 55 years old, and manufacturers did not have to start legally labeling their products as uniquely homemade until the 1960s when imports started to boom in American markets. To keep up with the costs of the cheaper imports, American manufacturers were forced to cut their own costs of production, decreasing their own quality as well. If you're looking for cast-iron, then pans from earlier eras, while more rare, will give you the best, handcrafted wares you could ever clean up and use.

Cast-iron cookware from this earlier time period, with a few exceptions, were typically labeled with the manufacturer, city and state of the foundry, a large number on the bottom or handle of the pan, and a small letter nearby the number. The number indicated what size woodstove eye the pan could fit, and the letter represents the pattern the pan was cast in (a misinformed seller may say these letters are the initialed name of a manufacturer).

There is a percentage of cast-iron that possesses neither manufacturer name nor their foundry location, making it an "unmarked" piece. These are just as well made as those that do have names; in most cases, manufacturers made these unmarked cookware for stores to sell at a lower price without sacrificing the value their name was associated with. For a period of years, certain manufacturers chose to use adhesive paper labels instead of casting their names into their wares, as well. In these cases, the pattern of the cast can usually be used to determine the company that forged it.

When cleaning a piece, you might find marks that appear worn off while the rest of the pan appears in a good, uncorroded condition. These are known as "ghost marks," and they are fairly common among old cast-iron pieces. Whenever manufacturers modified an existing pattern or their label, most of the time they simply filled in any pre-existing lettering and added new markings in their stead to use the same molds. This filler material would wear away faster than the rest of the mold, revealing a slight indentation where the previous label was. It's a unique little quirk that definitely gives your piece some history!

However, finding out an exact year your piece was made is difficult, if not impossible. Sometimes labels between years only differentiated by what font-type is used and even then the same label could be used in upwards a twenty-year span of manufacturing. An individual cast-iron will need personally tailored research if you're particularly curious in an estimated decade. You might find yourself with a surprise treasure in your possession!

CLEANING RUST AND REPAIRING SCRATCHES

Don't fret about finding a rusty pan! There are multiple techniques and products you can use in order to clean away rust. For all these methods, it's best to start with a fine-grain sandpaper to lightly buff off the rusted areas and get closer to the surface of the cast-iron. Here are a few of the easier methods to render your pan rust-free and ready:

A bath of 1 part white vinegar and 1 part water can remove surface rust after a good soak. Leave the cast-iron submerged for 30 minutes. You want the piece completely submerged or else the color will become uneven. Scrub the piece with a scouring pad or steel wool to loosen the rust off the pan. Depending on how much rust your cast-iron has, you may need to repeat the soak and scrub one more time. Don't leave the pan to soak for longer than 4 hours or else the acid in the vinegar will begin to damage the pan. Afterwards, thoroughly wash the pan in clean water, towel it off, allow it to dry completely, and season the pan as previously mentioned.

If you're feeling particularly thrifty, you can use a soak of Coca-Cola. The acid in the drink will break up the rust within 10 to 15 minutes and make it easier to scrub off, but you'll need to wash it in soapy water for this technique to get rid of the sticky sugar. Again, towel the cast-iron dry, allow it to dry completely, and proceed with the seasoning instructions found in the last chapter.

A molasses soak—while it takes longer (2 to 4 weeks) and needs a room temperature of 90 degrees—doesn't need any elbow grease afterwards, and will remove the rust within the nooks and crannies that would otherwise be very difficult to scrub out. For this, you need a liquid molasses, typically used for an animal feed supplement, so you'll probably find it easiest in your local farm supply store. You'll set up a bath of 1 part molasses to 9 parts water and submerge the piece in an upright position. It's recommended to do this outside; formation of mold and scum on the surface of this mixture is normal, and results in a particular odor you won't want indoors. Check it regularly to gauge progress, and once the piece is rust free, wash it thoroughly with hot water. Towel it off, allow it to dry completely, and proceed with the seasoning instructions found in the last chapter.

If your piece's surface is scratched, then you'll need a little more effort and more heavy-duty tools. Surface scratches can be buffed away with a high-grit sandpaper. Focus on a larger area than the scratch itself to prevent yourself from accidentally sanding a pit into the metal. If there are deeper scratches, then you can use a rotary tool and sanding disk. Blow off dust as you go, and rinse the pan when you've come to a scratch free surface. Let it dry completely, and proceed to season the pan to protect it.

CAST-IRON COOKWARE: THE CARE & KEEPING HANDBOOK

STRIPPING OLD SEASONING

Even if you find a rust-free pan, you probably want to strip the old seasoning. You don't know what that seasoning has previously been through, and it may not have been done correctly. Sellers sometimes hastily oil up a pan so that it has a nice sheen for display, but it may not have been oil you should cook with and may be difficult to clean afterwards.

The vinegar bath above will strip seasoning and you don't need a scrubbing pad or steel wool this time; a regular plastic scrub brush or sponge will work just fine. You can also try the market cast-iron or oven cleaners that advertise stripping. Just follow the printed instructions, and always re-season your pan after it's dry.

DISPLAY IT PROUDLY

If you find a piece that you'd like to display rather than cook with, collectors recommend using mineral oil as a protective coating. The directions for seasoning with this oil are a little different; the oven time and temperature are much shorter and lower than with regular seasoning because mineral oil's smoke point is much lower than cooking oils.

1. Place the stripped cast-iron upside down on the middle rack of the oven and preheat the oven to 200 degrees (with the pan inside). Once up to temp, turn the temperature up to 300 degrees.

2. If you want your iron darker, you can steadily raise the temperature to 500 degrees in 50-degree increments. Once at 500, turn the oven back down to 300. You may crack the door open to help the temperature drop. This is purely preferential, and is not a necessary step. If you do take this route, allow ample time for the pan to also return to 300 degrees. Applying mineral oil to a 400 or 500 degree pan will cause the oil to smoke.

3. Carefully remove the pan while still hot and apply a thin application of food grade mineral oil all over the surface. You can find this oil at the drug store; aim for a brand that has a "USP" label. Be very careful not to burn yourself!

4. Wipe off the excess oil and return the pan to the still-to-temp oven. Turn the oven off and allow the pan to cool in the oven.

If you ever want to repurpose a pan back into working, cooking order, just wash it with hot water and dishwashing liquid, then season the pan regularly with vegetable oil and the directions from the previous chapter.

HEARTH &
OUTDOORS
COOKING

Despite all the simplicity and versatility the cast-iron skillet adds to the modern kitchen, there's something truly satisfying to taking this cookware back to its roots. Open-fire cooking, either in your indoor hearth or an outdoor fire pit, has an intrinsic, colonial charm to it, and it's just plain fun to do. Those with a fireplace or fire pit are probably used to typical camping foods—hot dogs, potatoes wrapped in foil, perhaps chestnuts or popcorn, and of course, the famous s'more—but those foods can be made in a cast-iron skillet or Dutch oven both indoors and out. It's definitely an experience I'd recommend for a fun family evening in front of the fireplace on a cold winter's night or a warm summer gathered around the pit.

Practice makes perfect, but here are some pointers to consider before you begin cooking. As the Boy Scouts say: "Be prepared!"

HEAT SOURCE AND SETUP

Cooking directly on an open fire without a grate or on coals will actually burn your food. No, our aim is to get a good gathering of coals to cook on! Coals have a more consistent temperature for our skillet to soak up and distribute evenly to the meal. The more coals you put under a skillet or on a Dutch oven's lid, the hotter the interior will be.

A fire will be ready to cook with about 30-45 minutes after starting, when it can sustain itself without kindling and larger logs are producing plenty of warm coals to use. In preparing space for your skillet or Dutch oven, it's best to start your fire in only half of your hearth, campfire, or fire pit. Logs can still slow burn in one half while coals can be later moved to the second half to provide a flat, open space to cook. Coals will cool as you cook and new ones will have to replace the old; that's why you want to keep a small fire going as you cook! Try to break off similar sized coals so replacing them will maintain an even temperature.

Next, you want a level plane to cook on to prevent any possibly flammable spills. Coals smolder, shift, and break down, so you don't want to put a pan right on the coals. There are fairly basic camping grates you can stand within your coals, or you can more simply pick four similar sized, stable rocks to set your pan or Dutch oven upon. If you have a camping Dutch oven, then it should be made with three or four short legs already on the bottom of the vessel, and you won't need the grate or rocks.

COOKWARE

Both skillet and Dutch oven can be used on an open fire, but a Dutch oven's higher lip tends to be preferred to prevent spills or splashes, and its lid gives more options for heating and cooking. There are, of course, other case-iron devices that are useful in the campfire, such as pie irons or roasters.

Of Dutch ovens, there is either the home kitchen or camping varieties, and there

CAST-IRON COOKWARE: THE CARE & KEEPING HANDBOOK

are several differences that specialize these similar vessels to their unique tasks. The kitchen Dutch oven is flat bottomed with rounded lid, resembling a large stockpot. However, a camping Dutch oven is specialized with 3 or 4 legs cast onto the bottom of the vessel, as well as having a flat lid with a lip of 1-2 inches. This allows for coals to be placed on top to heat the inside, too—allowing for even convection within (cooking techniques are detailed below). A loop handle is commonly attached to the vessel, so that the pot can easily hang or be more easily pulled from the fire.

The other important tools are utensils. You're going to want metal tools, preferably some with some long handles that keep you a safe distance from the heat (with that in mind, do not use pans or pots with any rubber-coated handles). Despite the space a handle may afford you, always wear some heavy-duty gloves when cooking. Heat radiating close to coals can be upwards of 500-750 degrees, and this can quickly conduct up the handle of your utensil to your hand. Pliers are most useful to get the best leverage to remove the lid.

COOKING AND TEMPERATURE CONTROL

While skillet cooking is fairly straight forwards, Dutch oven cooking provides a variety of heating techniques to accomplish different methods of heating and preparing your meal. Here's how to best arrange your coals for certain types of cooking:

- For boiling, shallow frying, or deep fat frying, all heat should come from below, and thus, all coals should be placed underneath.

- For roasting, heat should be evenly distributed throughout the pot, so you want a 1-1 ratio of coals under and on top.

- For baking, more heat on top is preferred. Coals should be placed in a 1-3 ratio with the most on top of the lid.

- For simmering or stewing, more heat on the bottom is preferred. Coals should be placed below in a 4-1 ratio.

SAFETY TIPS

- When first learning how to cook on coals, water is your best device for learning how many coals equals a certain temperature. It gives a splendid visual based on when your skillet starts simmering or boiling, so practice with a few pans of shallow water to best understand how to control a skillet's temperature.

- Gradually heat up your cast-iron to prevent thermal shock, which may cause your cookware to warp. Simply place a room temperature skillet or Dutch oven near the fire to gain warmth before setting it upon the coals.

- Do not clean your cast-iron by burning it in the fire! This causes overheating of the cookware that can cause warping, cracking, or altering the metal's molecular structure, which may not allow it to hold onto a protective seasoning.

- Hardwoods, such as mesquite, ash, maple, hickory, and oak, hold heat for longer in their coals. Mesquite and hickory in particular can add additional flavor to your meal.

- Avoid cooking with yaupon, or holly wood, as it can make you sick.

- Be patient! It's better to take your time than have a burnt meal.

Be prepared to factor in carryover cooking, or cooking that occurs as the food is resting off the heat. An open fire and coals means more heat over a longer period of time, plus your cast-iron does a fantastic job of holding and distributing heat. This period can last up to 20 minutes, so remove your food just before you think you should and allow it time to rest before serving.

- Never use gasoline as a lighter fluid. Do not add lighter fluid to an already lit flame.

- Your fire should be at least 10 feet away from your home and in an open area without any overhanging awning or tree branches.

- Keep decorations away from your fire, such as plants, outdoor furniture, pillows, and umbrellas. These are very flammable due to their synthetic fibers, which burn easily and very quickly.

- Never leave your fire unattended, and keep children and pets at a safe distance.

- Avoid greasy or fatty foods when cooking in a skillet, as you don't want to accidentally cause a fat or grease fire. Any recipe that calls for oil is better in the Dutch oven, where the higher lip of the vessel protects from splatters getting into the fire. If a grease fire happens, never use water to put it out. This will cause the grease to splash, spreading the fire and potentially burning you. A bucket of sand is your next best option to smother the flames. Baking soda is commonly called on as a solution to a grease fire, but it probably won't be able to put out a large fire.

- Always be prepared for a fire. You should have a fire extinguisher on hand when an open flame is near, but should you lack one never use water to put out a grease fire!

- Seriously, get a fire extinguisher, know how to use it, and know when to replace it.

RECIPES FOR·GETTING STARTED

Be aware of is overall cooking time.
Because a cast-iron skillet is such a good
conductor of·heat, cooking times can
vary. The recipes indicate active and
overall times for the recipes, but some
assume basic prep work has already been
completed. I like to keep things simple
in my kitchen, so I tend to use the same
skillet for everything. It's a Lodge 12-inch
skillet and it's a fabulous pan. I also use
of my trusty 7-quart Dutch oven for some
bread recipes (pages 92-115).

BREAKFAST TREATS & PASTRIES

There's something about the very word breakfast that makes your mouth water in anticipation. The association with fried eggs, sizzling bacon, crisp-edged potatoes, butter melting over hot pancakes—flavors and aromas that jump-start your day and make you feel like you can tackle anything. Another reason a real breakfast is so satisfying is because it's not every day that we're able to indulge in it. Who has the time during the week to make pancakes—or even eggs? I suspect very few of us, which is why breakfast is particularly delicious and delightful when it can happen in our homes. The recipes in this chapter are what a good breakfast is all about—hearty, filling, hot, salty, sweet—or all of these things! Using cast-iron cookware to cook breakfast also connects you to a feeling of tradition. You can imagine pioneers and homesteaders reaching for their skillets while wondering what was next for them as they headed West. You can imagine a farmer's wife cracking just-gathered eggs into a hot skillet in anticipation of her husband and children finishing the first round of milking and chores on the dairy farm. In our kitchens and lives, surrounded by the latest technology, there's nothing like breakfast prepared in a cast-iron pan. So get cooking!

FRENCH TOAST

French toast—a great way to use up bread that's on the verge of going stale—is so simple and so satisfying.

6 eggs

1 cup milk

½ teaspoon
vanilla extract

Pinch of nutmeg,
if desired

6 slices thick-cut bread

4 to 6 tablespoons
butter

1. In a mixing bowl, combine the eggs, milk, vanilla, and nutmeg (if desired).

2. Place the slices of bread in a baking dish. Pour the egg mixture over the bread, shaking the pan to distribute evenly. Flip the pieces of bread a couple of times to coat both sides with the mixture.

3. Heat 2 tablespoons butter in the skillet over medium-high heat. Add 2 slices of bread to the pan and cook until golden brown on each side, 2 to 3 minutes a side. Transfer the cooked pieces to a warm plate or keep warm in the oven while you cook the additional pieces.

4. Serve with maple syrup or jam.

The secret to great French toast is the choice of bread and the amount of egg mixture that saturates the bread. If you use a basic sandwich bread, you won't need as much egg mixture. If you use an egg-based bread like Challah, or a sourdough bread, you'll need more egg mixture as these kinds of bread are denser. They will also need to sit in the egg mixture longer. You'll need to adjust the recipe for the type of bread you're using, so be sure to have some extra eggs and milk on hand.

DAVID EYRE'S PANCAKE

SERVES 4   **ACTIVE TIME: 30 MINUTES**   **START TO FINISH: 30 MINUTES**

A friend shared this recipe that she found in The New York Times *years ago. Turns out it has quite the following. It's more like a popover than a pancake, but it's really delicious. David Eyre was a writer/editor, so I'm happy to include this tribute to him and hopefully create a whole new following for it.*

½ cup flour

½ cup milk

2 eggs, lightly beaten

Pinch of nutmeg

4 tablespoons butter

2 tablespoons confectioner's sugar

Juice of half a lemon

Preheat oven to 425 degrees.

In a bowl, combine the flour, milk, eggs, and nutmeg. Beat lightly; leave the batter a little lumpy.

Melt the butter in the skillet and, when very hot, pour in the batter.

Transfer the skillet to the oven and bake for 15 to 20 minutes, until golden brown.

Sprinkle with the sugar, return briefly to the oven, then remove, sprinkle with lemon juice, and serve.

This "pancake" is usually served with jam, which leads to all kinds of flavor options. Try anything from a sweet strawberry jam to a more pungent orange marmalade or fig spread. In the fall, an apple or pear butter would be perfect.

APPLE PANCAKE

SERVES 4 TO 6 ✦ ACTIVE TIME: 30 MINUTES ✦ START TO FINISH: 60 MINUTES

Make this the morning after you go apple picking. It's a great way to use up some of the apples and get your day off to a great start.

4 eggs

1 cup milk

3 tablespoons sugar

½ teaspoon vanilla

½ teaspoon salt

¾ cup flour

4 tablespoons butter

2 apples, peeled, cored and thinly sliced

¼ teaspoon cinnamon

Dash of ground nutmeg

Dash of ground ginger

¼ cup light brown sugar

Confectioner's sugar for sprinkling (optional)

1. Preheat the oven to 425 degrees.

2. In a large bowl, whisk together the eggs, milk, sugar, vanilla, and salt. Add the flour and whisk to combine. Set the batter aside.

3. Heat the skillet over medium-high heat and add the butter, tilting the pan to thoroughly coat the bottom. Add the apple slices and top with the cinnamon, nutmeg, and ginger. Stir, cooking, until apples begin to soften, about 5 minutes. Add the brown sugar and continue to stir while cooking for an additional few minutes until apples are very soft. Pat the cooked apples along the bottom of the skillet to distribute evenly.

4. Pour the batter over the apples, coating them evenly. Transfer the skillet to the oven and bake for about 20 minutes until it is browned and puffed. Sprinkle with confectioner's sugar when fresh out of the oven if desired. Serve immediately.

You can vary the fruit-spice combo for this recipe in multiple ways. Consider making it with pears instead of apples, or using one of each. Add raisins to the apples or pears while cooking (about ½ cup), or try cranberries, blueberries, or dried cherries, along with toasted walnuts (about ½ cup).

BACON AND EGGS

SERVES 2 ✦ ACTIVE TIME: 20 MINUTES ✦ START TO FINISH: 30 MINUTES

Done right, a simple dish of sizzling bacon accompanied by fried eggs, their yolks golden and gooey, is a plate of heaven on earth.

8 slices bacon

4 eggs

1. Heat a 12-inch skillet over medium-high heat. As it is heating, lay the bacon strips side by side in the skillet. Cook for about 5 minutes a side or until the meaty parts are cooked through and the fatty parts are opaque. If you prefer your bacon extra crispy, keep an eye on it as it continues to cook and allow it to go another few minutes, turning after every couple of minutes.

2. Transfer the cooked bacon to a plate lined with paper towels, and keep it in a warm oven. Drain most of the fat from the skillet, but keep enough to coat the bottom.

3. The skillet should be hot from having just made the bacon. Crack the eggs into the sizzling bacon fat. Lower the heat to medium or low, and put a lid over the skillet for about 2 minutes to help cook the yolk without overdoing the white.

4. When the eggs are cooked, remove with a spatula and serve immediately, accompanied by the bacon.

We owe our American traditional breakfast of bacon and eggs to our English ancestors. A full English breakfast consists of eggs, sausage, potatoes, and even baked beans and tomatoes, all washed down with strong tea or coffee.

BEST-EVER HASH BROWNS

SERVES 4 TO 6 ✦ ACTIVE TIME: 40 MINUTES ✦ START TO FINISH: 60 MINUTES

I always ask for crispy hash browns when I order them in a diner because I love when the outside is crisp and browned and the inside is soft and hot. Even your favorite diner's preparation won't match this recipe, though.

4 large russet potatoes

1 yellow onion

1 teaspoon salt

½ teaspoon pepper, or to taste

4 tablespoons butter

1. Peel the potatoes and wash them to remove any dirt from the potato or your hands. Grate the potatoes using the large holes of a cheese grater. Put the grated potatoes in a mixing bowl.

2. Cut the onion in half, and using the fine holes of the cheese grater, grate the cut side of the onion over the potatoes so that some particles and juice go into the bowl. Don't overdo the onion; a couple of swipes over the grater is a good start. Thoroughly combine the potatoes and onion.

3. Squeeze the grated vegetables through a cheesecloth or in some paper towels. You want to get them as dry as possible. Stir in the salt and pepper.

4. Heat the butter in the skillet over medium-high heat until bubbling. Add the potatoes, pressing the mixture into the bottom of the pan to form a large pancake. Cook for 4 to 5 minutes on one side, then flip the potatoes and cook for another 3 minutes or more on the other side, depending on how crisp you want the potatoes. If you want to cook them a little longer, consider adding some more butter to the pan, one tablespoon at a time.

5. Serve hot, seasoning with additional salt and pepper if desired.

If you have a food processor, you can use the shredding blade instead of using a cheese grater for the potatoes. The finer your shreds, the faster the potatoes will cook. Consider cooking them in bacon grease instead of butter for added flavor.

CORNED BEEF HASH

SERVES 4 TO 6 ✦ ACTIVE TIME: 40 MINUTES ✦ START TO FINISH: 90 MINUTES

If you like to eat this at a diner, wait until you make it yourself. It's so good!

2 large russet
potatoes, peeled
and cut into cubes

1 teaspoon salt

3 tablespoons butter

1 Vidalia onion, diced

3 cloves garlic, minced

1 red bell pepper,
cored and seeded,
chopped fine

1 pound corned
beef, cut into
bite-sized pieces

½ teaspoon
dried thyme

Salt and freshly
ground pepper
to taste

1. Put the potatoes in a saucepan and cover with cold water. Add the salt. Bring the water to a boil, then lower the heat and cook the potatoes about 10 minutes until partially cooked. (Cooking until soft will cause them to fall apart in the hash.) Drain them in a colander and rinse with cold water. Set aside.

2. Heat the butter in the skillet over medium-high heat. Add the onions, garlic, and pepper and cook, stirring, until the vegetables soften, about 3 minutes.

3. Add the potatoes and press them down into the skillet around the vegetables. Allow them to set and cook for about 5 minutes, then start turning sections over with a spatula while stirring in the corned beef. Sprinkle with the thyme, and season with salt and pepper. Continue to cook for about 5 minutes so that the potatoes are browned and the corned beef is warmed through. Season with additional salt and pepper if desired.

If you like eggs with your corned beef hash, once the potatoes are browned, make 4 to 6 indentations in the top of the hash and break the eggs into them. Lower the heat and cover the skillet. Continue cooking until the eggs are set, about 3 minutes.

EGGS IN A NEST

SERVES 2 ✦ ACTIVE TIME: 20 MINUTES ✦ START TO FINISH: 40 MINUTES

This is a dish that's as much about presentation as it is about taste, but both are fabulous. It's guaranteed to put a smile on your child's face in the morning.

4 pieces of sandwich bread

4 tablespoons butter

4 eggs

Salt and pepper to taste

1. Toast the bread on the light setting of the toaster, until it is just browned. Using a cookie cutter or the top of a small glass, perforate a hole in the center of the piece of toast.

2. Heat 2 tablespoons of the butter in the skillet over medium-high heat. Put two pieces of the toast with the holes in it in the pan. Cook for a couple of minutes on one side to get them golden, then flip the toasts.

3. Crack the eggs into the holes. Lower the heat slightly, cover the pan, and cook until the egg is set, about 3 minutes. Serve the cooked pieces and repeat the cooking process with the other pieces of toast and eggs. Season with salt and pepper before serving.

Using cookie cutters of different shapes can be fun and festive, too.

CHEESY GRITS

SERVES 4 TO 6 ✦ ACTIVE TIME: 20 MINUTES ✦ START TO FINISH: 40 MINUTES

Done right, grits are a mouthful of special. No wonder they're a regular on the breakfast plates of Southerners.

2 cups whole milk

2 cups water

1 cup grits

1 teaspoon salt

1 teaspoon pepper

2 cups grated cheddar cheese (packed)

1. Preheat the broiler to high.

2. Bring the milk and water to a boil. Add the grits and stir, cooking constantly, until grits are thickened and cooked, about 15 minutes. Add the salt and pepper and 1 cup of the cheese. Stir to combine.

3. Grease the skillet with some butter and add the grits. Sprinkle with the remaining cup of cheese. Put the skillet in the oven and allow the grits to toast under the broiler, about 2 minutes. Serve immediately.

If you want spicier grits, use 1 cup Pepper Jack cheese as half of the cheese you include. Or try other hard cheeses like Swiss, mozzarella, or fresh Parmesan.

SAVORY SCONES

SERVES 4 TO 6 ✦ ACTIVE TIME: 30 MINUTES ✦ START TO FINISH: 50 MINUTES

These cheesy scones with extra black pepper are a nice complement to scrambled eggs. You can also split them and use them as sandwich bread for a ham-and-egg breakfast sandwich. Or enjoy them in the afternoon with a cup of tea.

2 cups flour

1 teaspoon baking powder

½ teaspoon salt

1 teaspoon freshly ground black pepper

½ teaspoon dry mustard

4 tablespoons butter, chilled, cut into pieces

½ cup grated sharp cheddar cheese

½ cup milk

1 egg beaten with a little milk

1. Preheat oven to 400 degrees. Position a rack in the middle of the oven.

2. In a large bowl, whisk together the flour, baking powder, salt, pepper, and dry mustard. Add the butter pieces and mix with a fork to form a crumbly dough.

3. Stir in the cheese and milk. With flour on your hands, transfer the dough to a lightly floured surface.

4. Form the dough into a circle about ½-inch thick. With a long knife, cut the dough into 6 to 8 wedges.

5. Butter the skillet, and put the scone wedges in a circle in it, leaving some space between the pieces.

6. Brush with the beaten egg. Bake for 20 to 25 minutes, or until golden.

For an added breakfast treat, include bacon bits in the dough. Add about ⅓ cup crumbled bacon or bacon bits to the dough when adding the cheese and milk.

ALMOND COFFEE CAKE

SERVES 6 TO 8 ✦ ACTIVE TIME: 90 MINUTES ✦ START TO FINISH: 2 HOURS

Toasted almonds and almond extract impart a heavenly taste and fragrance to this traditional morning cake.

Cake
1¾ cups flour

⅔ cup sugar

½ teaspoon baking soda

¼ teaspoon salt

8 tablespoons butter, softened

2 eggs

1 teaspoon almond extract

½ cup buttermilk

Topping
½ cup sugar

½ cup dark brown sugar

½ teaspoon ginger

¼ teaspoon salt

12 tablespoons (1½ sticks) unsalted butter, melted

2 cups flour

½ cup dried organic coconut

1. Preheat the oven to 325 degrees.

2. To make the cake, whisk together the flour, sugar, baking soda, and salt in a large bowl. Add the butter and stir with an electric mixer until blended.

3. In a small bowl, whisk together the eggs, almond extract, and buttermilk. Pour into the flour mixture and blend on high speed until the batter is light and fluffy. Pour the batter into a greased skillet.

4. To make the topping, whisk together the sugars, ginger, and salt in a bowl. Add the melted butter and combine. Then add the flour and coconut and stir to form a crumbly dough.

5. Dot the topping over the cake in the skillet. Put the skillet in the oven and bake for 45 minutes, until knife inserted in the middle comes out clean. Allow to cool for about 10 minutes before serving.

Fresh fruit is a great addition to this coffeecake. Before putting on the topping, sprinkle in some peeled, chopped pears, or some blueberries, or pears and cranberries.

CINNAMON BUNS

SERVES 6 ✦ ACTIVE TIME: 60 MINUTES ✦ START TO FINISH: 90 MINUTES

There's something about serving these fresh out of the skillet that makes them even more special than they already are. If you love the smell (and taste) of cinnamon, you will gobble these up.

26.4-oz. package(s) frozen biscuits

All-purpose flour for dusting

2 teaspoons ground cinnamon

¾ cup firmly packed dark brown sugar

4 tablespoons butter, softened

1 cup confectioner's sugar

3 tablespoons half-and-half

½ teaspoon vanilla extract

1. Preheat oven to 375 degrees.

2. Lightly dust a flat surface with flour. Spread the frozen biscuit dough out in rows of 4 biscuits each. Cover with a dishcloth and let sit for about 30 minutes until the dough is thawed but still cool.

3. Mix the cinnamon and brown sugar in a small bowl.

4. When the dough is ready, sprinkle flour over the top and fold it in half, then press it out to form a large rectangle (approximately 10x12 inches). Spread the softened butter over the dough, then the cinnamon/sugar mix. Roll up the dough, starting with a long side. Cut into 1-inch slices and place in a lightly greased skilled.

5. Bake at 375 degrees for about 35 minutes, until rolls in the center are cooked through. Remove from the oven and allow to cool slightly.

6. Make the glaze by mixing the confectioner's sugar, half-and-half, and vanilla. Drizzle over the warm rolls and serve.

Cinnamon is a spice with a long history of health benefits as well as culinary delights. The cinnamon sticks sold in stores are actually "quills" from cinnamon trees; they're the inner bark. Cinnamon is grown in India, Sri Lanka, Indonesia, Madagascar, Brazil, and parts of the Caribbean. Its smell is said to invigorate cognitive functions, and its compounds have antibacterial and analgesic properties. Cinnamon is used in both sweet and savory dishes.

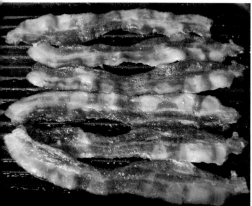

CRUSTS & BREADS

Wait until you taste the mouthwatering breads and delectable pies that will be coming out of your oven when you start baking with the cast-iron skillet! You'll find that things are cooked more evenly, yielding the best-tasting breads, pies, and more. This chapter includes some basic breads and a useful crust for later recipes that are sure to be family favorites—even gluten-free options!

FLAKY PASTRY CRUST

This is the traditional pie crust recipe, and while it's tempting to take a shortcut and use a pie crust mix or even a pre-made crust, there truly is nothing as delicious as a crust made from scratch. Once you get the hang of it, too, you'll find making the crust as enjoyable and therapeutic as indulging in the pie.

2½ cups flour

1 teaspoon salt

¼ cup vegetable shortening

½ cup (1 stick) butter, chilled and cut into small pieces (if using unsalted butter, increase salt to 1¼ teaspoons), plus 1 tablespoon butter for greasing the skillet

6 to 8 tablespoons cold water

1 tablespoon milk

1. In a large bowl, combine the flour and salt. Add the shortening, and using a fork, work it in until the mixture forms very coarse meal. Add the butter and work into the dough with a pastry blender or your fingers until the meal is just holding together. Don't overwork the dough; there can be chunks of butter in it. Add 4 tablespoons cold water to start, and using your hands or a fork, work the dough, adding additional tablespoons until it just holds together when you gather it in your hands.

2. Working on a lightly floured surface, gather the dough and place it on the work area, forming it into a solid ball. Separate into equal parts and form into disks. Wrap each tightly in plastic wrap and refrigerate for 30 to 60 minutes. Dough can be refrigerated for a couple of days or frozen for a couple of months.

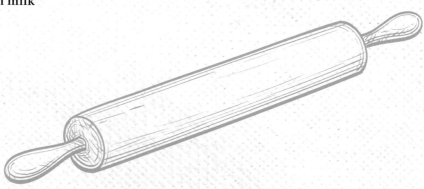

3. Take the dough out of the refrigerator to allow it to warm up a bit but work with it cold. Put the refrigerated dough on a lightly floured surface, and with a lightly dusted rolling pin, flatten the dough into 2 circles, working both sides to extend each to a 10- to 12-inch round.

4. Grease the cast-iron skillet with 1 tablespoon of butter.

5. Carefully position the crust in the skillet so it is evenly distributed, pressing it in lightly and allowing the dough to extend over the side.

6. If making a single-crust pie, crimp the edges as desired. If filling and adding a top crust, leave the extra dough so it can be crimped with the top crust. Fill the pie as directed, and then roll out the top crust so it is just bigger than the diameter of the top of the skillet. For an extra flaky pastry crust, refrigerate the completed pie for about 30 minutes before baking.

7. When ready to bake, cut a slit or hole in the middle of the top crust for heat to escape. Brush the crust with milk, which will turn it a nice brown color. Bake as directed.

GLUTEN-FREE CRUST

MAKES 1 12-INCH CRUST ✦ ACTIVE TIME: 20 MINUTES ✦ START TO FINISH: 90 MINUTES

Achieving something somewhat flaky is the trick with a gluten-free piecrust. This comes very close, and it's delicious, too. Double the recipe for a two-crust pie.

1¼ cups gluten-free multi-purpose flour blend

1 tablespoon sugar

½ teaspoon xanthan gum

½ teaspoon salt

6 tablespoons unsalted butter, chilled and cut into small pieces, plus 1 tablespoon butter for greasing the skillet

1 large egg

2 teaspoons fresh squeezed lemon juice

1 to 2 tablespoons cold water

1. In a large bowl, combine the flour blend, sugar, xanthan gum, and salt. Add the butter and work it into the flour mixture with a pastry blender or your fingers to form a coarse meal that includes whole bits of butter.

2. In a small bowl, whisk the egg and lemon juice together briskly until very foamy. Add to the dry ingredients and stir until the dough holds together. If dough isn't quite holding, add 1 tablespoon of cold water at a time until it does. Shape into a disk, wrap tightly in plastic wrap, and refrigerate for 30 to 60 minutes or overnight.

3. When ready to make the pie, take dough out of the refrigerator and allow to rest at room temperature for about 10 minutes before rolling. Working on a flat surface dusted with gluten-free flour, roll the dough into a 12-inch disk.

4. Grease the cast-iron skillet with 1 tablespoon of butter.

5. Carefully position the crust in the skillet so it is evenly distributed, pressing it in lightly. Crimp the edges. Fill and bake as directed.

CORNBREAD

MAKES 4 TO 6 SERVINGS   ACTIVE TIME: 1 HOUR
START TO FINISH: 3 TO 4 HOURS

If you're going to make bread in a cast-iron skillet, you have to make corn bread. In fact, many restaurants serve cornbread in a cast-iron dish.

4 cups finely ground yellow cornmeal

¾ cup sugar

1 tablespoon salt

4 cups boiling water

1 cup flour

1 tablespoon butter, melted

2 eggs, lightly beaten

2 teaspoons baking powder

1 teaspoon baking soda

1 cup milk

1 teaspoon butter

In a large bowl, combine cornmeal, sugar, salt, and boiling water. Stir to combine and let sit for several hours in a cool, dark place or overnight in the refrigerator. Stir occasionally while batter rests.

When ready to make, preheat oven to 450 degrees.

Add flour, melted butter, eggs, baking powder, baking soda, and milk. Stir to thoroughly combine.

Heat the skillet over medium-high heat and melt the teaspoon of butter in it. Add the batter.

Transfer the skillet to the oven and cook for 15 minutes.

Reduce the heat to 250 degrees and cook another 40 minutes or until golden brown on the top and set in the center.

Cornbread recipes are as varied and plentiful as those for chili. A fun way to discover different ones that you like without having to go through multiple cookbooks and lots of time in the kitchen yourself is to invite friends and family to a Cast-Iron Cornbread Cook-Off. Make the chili the way you like it (and plenty of it), then have people bring over their cornbreads with recipes.

CREPES

These are very thin pancakes that can be filled with any number of things. The batter can be made with or without sugar, depending on whether you want to fill them with savory or sweet ingredients. Making them for the first time is intimidating, as it involves getting a hang of the right amount of batter on the skillet that's heated to the right temperature, but once you get the hang of it, it's a very satisfying experience that yields great results!

4 tablespoons melted butter

3 eggs

⅛ teaspoon salt

1 cup whole milk (possibly more)

1 cup flour (minus 2 tablespoons)

1. Heat the skillet over low heat to melt 2 tablespoons of the butter very slowly.

2. In a large mixing bowl, whisk the eggs until smooth. Add the salt and milk and whisk together until well blended. Whisk in the flour and, while whisking, add 2 tablespoons of the melted butter. Keep whisking until the batter is smooth and there are no lumps. Cover the bowl with plastic wrap or a clean dishtowel, put in a cool, dark place, and let rest for 3 or 4 hours before making the crepes.

3. You'll need a spatula that won't scratch the surface of the skillet. Have that and a ladle for scooping out the batter ready by the stove.

4. Heat the skillet over medium-high heat and melt a slice of the remaining 2 tablespoons of butter in it. Stir the crepe batter to blend again. When the skillet is hot but not smoking (the butter should not brown), use the ladle to scoop about ¼ cup into the skillet. When the batter hits the pan, tilt it gently to spread the batter evenly over the bottom. When the bottom is covered, cook for just over 1 minute and then flip the crepe over and cook the other side for about half the time. Tilt the skillet over a plate to slide the crepe out.

5. You should be able to make several crepes per slice of butter, but gauge the pan by how dry it is, and if you think it needs butter, add some. If the pan gets too hot and the butter browns, wipe it out with a paper towel and start over.

6. Continue making the crepes until all the batter is used up. As they cool on the plate, put pieces of waxed paper between them to keep them from sticking together. If you're not going to use them right away, wrap the stack in aluminum foil and keep them in the refrigerator or freeze them.

Variations

- To make dessert crepes, add 3 tablespoons of sugar when you add the flour, and 2 tablespoons Cognac (or 1 tablespoon vanilla) once the batter is mixed.

- Fill savory crepes with a variety of cooked meats, poultry, or fish, in a sauce. For example, you can use pieces of leftover chicken in a cream sauce with peas and mushrooms. Roll a generous spoonful up in the crepe, tuck it into a baking dish (with others), sprinkle with shredded cheese and bake in the oven at 350 degrees for about 10 minutes.

- Cook some spicy Italian sausage, spread some ricotta on the crepe, add the sausage, season with salt and pepper, roll up and put in a baking dish, cover with marinara and shredded mozzarella, and bake at 350 degrees for about 15 minutes.

BASIC WHITE BREAD

MAKES 1 SMALL ROUND ✦ ACTIVE TIME: 25 MINUTES ✦
START TO FINISH: 3 HOURS

I was skeptical of the recipes I found for baking bread in a cast-iron Dutch oven. They called for heating the cookware in the oven while the oven preheated (to a very high 450 degrees) and leaving the lid on for part of the baking time. But the photos looked good, so I dove in. This was the first recipe I made, and it was a great success and huge hit. I'm definitely a convert. Hope you will be, too. I used a 7-quart cast-iron Dutch oven for this recipe.

¼ teaspoon active
dry yeast

¼ teaspoon sugar

1½ cups water
(110 to 115 degrees)

1 teaspoon kosher salt

3 cups all-purpose
flour plus more for
kneading and dusting

1. Put the yeast and sugar in a measuring cup and add about ½ cup warm water in a drizzle. Hot water will kill the yeast, so it's important that the water be warm without being hot. Cover the measuring cup with plastic wrap and set it aside for about 15 minutes. If the yeast doesn't foam, it is not alive and you'll need to start over.

2. When the yeast is proofed, pour it into a large bowl and add the additional cup of warm water. Stir gently to combine. Add the salt to the flour, and add the flour to the yeast mixture. Stir with a wooden spoon until combined. The dough will be wet and sticky.

3. Put a dusting of flour on a flat surface and lift out the dough. With flour on your hands and more at the ready, begin kneading the dough so that it loses its stickiness. Don't overdo it, and don't use too much flour; just enough that it is more cohesive.

4. Place the dough in a large bowl, cover the bowl with plastic wrap, and allow to rise untouched for at least one hour, and up to several hours. Gently punch it down, recover with the plastic, and allow to rise again for another 30 minutes or so.

5. While the dough is on its final rise, preheat the oven to 450 degrees. Put a piece of parchment paper on the bottom of the Dutch oven and put it in with the lid on so it gets hot. When the oven is ready and dough has risen, carefully

remove the lid and gently scoop the dough from the bowl into the pot. Cover and bake for 15 minutes. Remove the lid and continue to bake for another 15 to 20 minutes until the top is golden and it sounds hollow when tapped.

6. Remove the pot from the oven and use tea towels to carefully remove the bread. Allow to cool before slicing.

It's important to "proof" the yeast before adding it to your recipe to ensure that it is fresh and active. If it is, it reacts with the sugar and liquid and creates tiny bubbles. It also releases a smell that is described (appropriately enough) as "yeasty"— the smell you get from fresh-baked bread. Yeast reacts with sugar to release carbon dioxide and, eventually, alcohol. This is the basis of making beer and wine, too. But with baking, the fermentation process stops when the live cells are cooked in the oven.

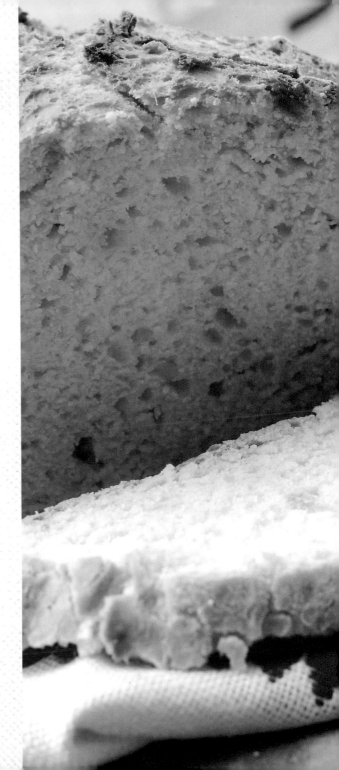

GLUTEN-FREE BREAD

**MAKES 1 SMALL ROUND ✦ ACTIVE TIME: 25 MINUTES ✦
START TO FINISH: 3 HOURS**

*I used a 7-quart cast-iron Dutch oven for this recipe. We are fortunate to live in a
time when gluten-free options are numerous. If you love bread and can't or don't want
to eat gluten, make this recipe and dig in! You'll be amazed at the result—an equally
crusty yet fluffy loaf that tastes great!*

½ teaspoon
instant yeast

¼ teaspoon sugar

1½ to 2½ cups water
(110 to 115 degrees)

1 teaspoon kosher salt

1½ teaspoons
xanthan gum

3 cups Bob's Red Mill
gluten-free flour plus
more for kneading
and dusting

⅓ cup Bob's Red
Mill sweet rice flour
(glutinous rice flour)

1. Put the yeast and sugar in a measuring cup and add about
   ½ cup warm water in a drizzle. Hot water will kill the yeast,
   so it's important that the water be warm without being hot.
   Cover the measuring cup with plastic wrap and set it aside
   for about 15 minutes. If the yeast doesn't foam, it is not alive
   and you'll need to start over.

2. When the yeast is proofed, pour it into a large bowl and
   add an additional cup of warm water. Stir gently to combine.
   Add the salt and xanthan gum to the flour, and add the flour
   to the yeast mixture. Stir with a wooden spoon until
   combined. Add up to an additional cup of warm water to
   accommodate the rice flour, which is tackier than regular
   flour. The dough should be wet and sticky.

3. Put a dusting of flour on a flat surface and lift out the dough.
   With flour on your hands and more at the ready, begin
   kneading the dough so that it loses its stickiness. Don't
   overdo it, and don't use too much flour; just enough that
   it is more cohesive.

4. Place the dough in a large bowl, cover the bowl with plastic wrap, and allow to rise untouched for at least one hour, and up to several hours. Gently punch it down, recover with the plastic, and allow to rise again for another 30 minutes or so.

5. While the dough is on its final rise, preheat the oven to 450 degrees. Put a piece of parchment paper on the bottom of the Dutch oven and put it in with the lid on so it gets hot. When the oven is ready and dough has risen, carefully remove the lid and gently scoop the dough from the bowl into the pot. Cover and bake for 15 minutes. Remove the lid and continue to bake for another 15 to 20 minutes until the top is golden and it sounds hollow when tapped.

6. Remove the pot from the oven and use tea towels to carefully remove the bread. Allow to cool before slicing.

WHEAT BREAD

I used a 7-quart cast-iron Dutch oven for this recipe. When you discover how easy it is to make such a tasty loaf of bread with all-purpose flour, you'll want to start experimenting with other flavors and textures, found in flours, nuts, and so on. Here's a wheat bread recipe that uses enough all-purpose flour to ensure adequate rising and fluffiness upon baking.

¼ teaspoon
instant yeast

¼ teaspoon **sugar**

1½ cups **water**
(110 to 115 degrees)

1 teaspoon **kosher salt**

2 cups **whole-wheat flour**

1 cup **all-purpose flour** plus more for kneading and dusting

1. Put the yeast and sugar in a measuring cup and add about ½ cup warm water in a drizzle. Hot water will kill the yeast, so it's important that the water be warm without being hot. Cover the measuring cup with plastic wrap and set it aside for about 15 minutes. If the yeast doesn't foam, it is not alive and you'll need to start over.

2. When the yeast is proofed, pour it into a large bowl and add the additional cup of warm water. Stir gently to combine. Add the salt to the flour, and add the flour to the yeast mixture. Stir with a wooden spoon until combined. The dough will be wet and sticky.

3. Put a dusting of flour on a flat surface and lift out the dough. With flour on your hands and more at the ready, begin kneading the dough so that it loses its stickiness. Don't overdo it, and don't use too much flour; just enough that it is more cohesive.

4. Place the dough in a large bowl, cover the bowl with plastic wrap, and allow to rise untouched for at least one hour, and up to several hours. Gently punch it down, recover with the plastic, and allow to rise again for another 30 minutes or so.

5. While the dough is on its final rise, preheat the oven to 450 degrees. Put a piece of parchment paper on the bottom of the Dutch oven and put it in with the lid on so it gets hot. When the oven is ready and dough has risen, carefully remove the lid and gently scoop the dough from the bowl into the pot. Cover and bake for 15 minutes. Remove the lid and continue

to bake for another 15 to 20 minutes until the top is golden and it sounds hollow when tapped.

6. Remove the pot from the oven and use tea towels to carefully remove the bread. Allow to cool before slicing.

Variations

❋ Making this with a seeded crust really boosts the flavor and adds texture, too. A nice combination is toasted sesame seeds with poppy seeds. When the dough is in the Dutch oven and ready to be baked, sprinkle generously with the seeds, pressing just lightly to help the seeds adhere.

❋ **Gluten-Free Variation:** Make a gluten-free whole grain loaf by mixing one 20-ounce bag of Bob's Red Mill Hearty Whole Grain Bread mix with 1¾ cup water, 2 eggs, ¼ cup vegetable oil, and 2 teaspoons cider vinegar. There's an envelope of yeast in the package. Allow it to proof in the water, mix in the other ingredients, knead, and allow to rise about 45 minutes before baking in the Dutch oven as you would for the Wheat Bread recipe.

IRISH SODA BREAD

MAKES 1 LOAF ✦ ACTIVE TIME: 30 MINUTES ✦ START TO FINISH: 90 MINUTES

Make this on a weekend morning when you have some extra time, then have slices of it later in the day with a cup of coffee or tea.

4 cups flour

½ cup sugar

⅛ teaspoon salt

3¼ teaspoons baking powder

½ teaspoon baking soda

2 tablespoons caraway seeds

2 large eggs, lightly beaten

1½ cups buttermilk

8 oz. golden raisins

1. Preheat the oven to 450 degrees.

2. Combine the flour, sugar, salt, baking powder, baking soda, and caraway seeds. Add the beaten eggs and stir to combine. Gradually add the buttermilk until the dough is sticky and messy. Stir in the raisins.

3. Generously butter the cast-iron skillet, and scoop and spread the dough in it.

4. Bake for about 1 hour, until the top is crusty and brown and the bread sounds hollow when tapped. Insert a toothpick in the center, too, to be sure the dough is cooked through. It should come out clean.

5. Serve with fresh butter and orange marmalade.

It wouldn't be St. Patrick's Day without Irish Soda bread. According to the Culinary Institute of America, "With a history spanning more than two centuries, soda bread is a traditional Irish specialty. The first loaf, consisting of little more than flour, baking soda, salt, and sour milk, made its debut in the mid-1800s when baking soda found its way into Irish kitchens." They don't mention the raisins or caraway seeds, but I consider these essential!

BISCUITS

For fluffy biscuits, you need to work with a very hot skillet. The golden brown crust on the bottom is as much of a delight as the airy, warm dough.

2 cups flour

1 teaspoon sugar

1 teaspoon salt

1 tablespoon baking powder

6 to 8 tablespoons butter, cut into pieces

½ cup + 2 tablespoons buttermilk

1. Preheat oven to 450 degrees.

2. In a large bowl, combine the flour, sugar, salt, and baking powder.

3. Using a fork or pastry knife, blend in 6 tablespoons of the butter to form crumbly dough. Form a well in the middle and add ½ cup buttermilk. Stir to combine and form a stiff dough. Using your fingers works best! If it seems too dry, add 1 tablespoon more of the buttermilk, going to 2 tablespoons if necessary.

4. Put 2 tablespoons butter in the skillet and put it in the oven to melt while the skillet heats.

5. Put the dough on a lightly floured surface and press out to a thickness of about 1 inch. Press out biscuits using an inverted water glass. Place the biscuits in the skillet and bake for about 10 minutes, until golden on the bottom.

Biscuits are another buttery bread that can be served with savory or sweet additions. You can make mini ham sandwiches by splitting the biscuits, putting some mayonnaise and grainy mustard on them, and putting in a slice of fresh-baked ham. You can fill them with scrambled eggs and bacon bits. Or you can slather them with butter and your favorite jam or honey. Or just eat them as-is.

GLUTEN-FREE BISCUITS

SERVES 4 TO 6 ✦ ACTIVE TIME: 20 MINUTES ✦ START TO FINISH: 40 MINUTES

It is possible to make delicious gluten-free biscuits, though they'll be a bit more crumbly than those made with regular flour.

1½ cups rice flour

⅓ cup potato starch

3 tablespoons tapioca flour

1 tablespoon baking powder

3 teaspoons maple sugar, or 1 tablespoon maple syrup

2 teaspoons cream of tartar

¼ teaspoon salt

1 teaspoon xanthan gum

5 to 7 tablespoons butter

½ cup + 2 tablespoons buttermilk

1. Preheat oven to 450 degrees.

2. In a large bowl, combine the flours, baking powder, sugar, cream of tartar, salt, and xanthan gum. Using a fork or pastry knife, blend in 5 tablespoons of the butter to form crumbly dough.

3. Form a well in the middle and add ½ cup buttermilk. Stir to combine and form a stiff dough. Using your fingers works best! If it seems too dry, add 1 tablespoon more of the buttermilk, going to 2 tablespoons if necessary.

4. Put 2 tablespoons butter in the skillet and put it in the oven to melt while the skillet heats.

5. Put the dough on a lightly floured surface and press out to a thickness of about 1 inch. Press out biscuits using an inverted water glass. Place the biscuits in the skillet and bake for about 10 minutes, until golden on the bottom.

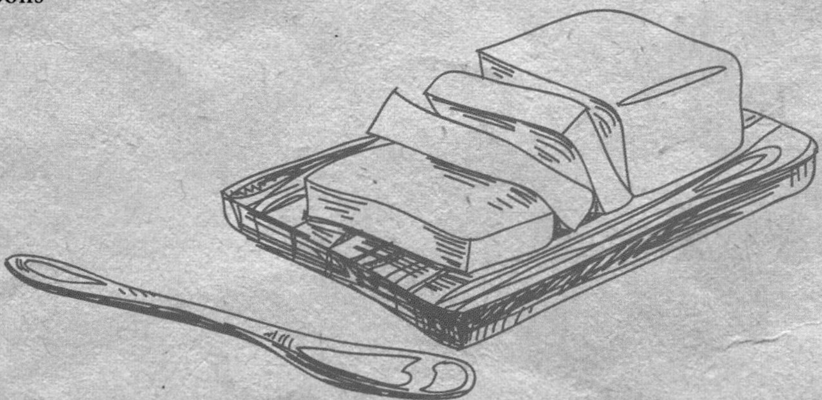

ENTREES

When you're looking for something that's loaded with flavor to be the centerpiece of your meal, start in this chapter. The cast-iron skillet's versatility and practicality shine through when used to cook meats, fish, and casseroles. You'll find everything here from amazing crab cakes to simple meat-and-veggie-stuffed pot pies and satisfyingly juicy meats. The cast-iron skillet does an amazing job of browning on the outside while retaining moisture on the inside. It can go from stove to oven and handle the heat from both, which means there are fewer pans and dishes to fuss with when you're preparing a main course. And so, without further ado, here are some recipes to whet your appetite and excite your senses.

CHICKEN POT PIE

MAKES 1 LOAF ✦ ACTIVE TIME: 30 MINUTES ✦ START TO FINISH: 90 MINUTES

When you have leftover chicken, reach for this recipe.

1 crust recipe
for a single crust
(see page 94 or 96)

2 tablespoons olive oil

½ yellow onion, diced

1 clove garlic, chopped

1 carrot, peeled and
cut into thin rounds

2 tablespoons butter,
cut into smaller slices

2 tablespoons flour

1¼ cups milk at
room temperature

1½ cups cooked
chicken, cut into
bite-sized pieces

¾ cup frozen green
bean pieces

Salt and pepper
to taste

½ teaspoon
cayenne (optional)

1 tablespoon
half-and-half

1. Preheat the oven to 350 degrees.

2. In a small skillet (not the cast-iron skillet), heat the olive oil. Add the onion and garlic and stir, cooking, for about 2 minutes. Add the carrot slices. Reduce the heat to low and cook, covered, stirring occasionally, until the carrots start to soften and the onions caramelize, about 5 minutes. Set aside.

3. Before starting to make the white sauce, be sure the milk is at room temperature. If it's not, microwave it so that it's just warm, about 15 to 20 seconds. Have the milk ready.

4. In the cast-iron skillet, over medium heat, melt the butter. Sprinkle the flour over it and stir quickly yet gently to blend the flour in with the butter. Reduce the heat slightly so the butter doesn't burn. Stir until the butter and flour are combined, a minute or so. They will form a soft paste.

5. Add just a little of the warm milk and stir constantly to blend it in. Add more milk in small increments, working after each addition to stir it into the flour and butter mixture smoothly. Work this way until all the milk has been incorporated. Continue to stir the sauce, cooking over low heat, until it thickens, about 5 minutes.

6. Add the chicken pieces, green beans, and vegetable mixture from the other skillet. Season with salt and pepper. If you want a hint of heat, add the cayenne pepper.

7. On a lightly floured surface, roll out the crust so it will fit over the filling. Lay it gently on top, push down slightly to secure, and cut 3 or 4 slits in the middle. Brush the crust with the half-and-half.

8. Put the skillet in the oven and bake for 30 to 40 minutes, until the crust is browned and the filling is bubbly.

9. Allow to cool slightly before serving.

PIZZA

This is breadmaking at its simplest: flour, water, salt, and yeast. There's actually a cookbook with that title! With this super-easy recipe, you can create amazing pizzas that can be completely individualized with almost anything you have in the fridge or pantry, from traditional cheese to "gourmet." And while the flavor will become more complex and the crust crispier if you allow the dough to rise for a couple of hours (or up to 3 days in the refrigerator), you can also roll it out and bake it within 15 minutes of making it.

¾ cup water
(110 to 115 degrees)

1 teaspoon active
dry yeast

2 cups all-purpose
flour

1½ teaspoons salt

1 tablespoon olive oil

Toppings
Traditional pizza toppings include the base of marinara topped with mozzarella cheese, as well as ricotta cheese, Italian seasonings, garlic, fresh tomatoes, pepperoni, sausage, meatballs, spinach, olives, mushrooms, peppers, onions— almost anything!

If you'll be making pizza within the hour, preheat the oven to 450 degrees.

In a large bowl, add the warm water and yeast, stirring to dissolve the yeast. Stir in the flour and salt and mix until the dough is just combined. It will be sticky.

Turn out on a floured surface and start kneading until the flour is incorporated, adding more if necessary until the dough is malleable and smooth, but not overdone.

Allow the dough to rest for 15 minutes. While it's doing so, put the skillet in the oven to get hot. Prepare the toppings for the pizza.

After 15 minutes or when ready, put a piece of parchment paper under the dough. Start rolling and pushing it out to form a 9-inch disk that will fit in the skillet. If it bounces back, let it rest before pushing or rolling it out again.

When the disk is formed, use pot holders or oven mitts to remove the skillet from the oven. Add the olive oil and brush to distribute over the bottom. Transfer the dough to the skillet and add the toppings.

Bake for 12 to 15 minutes until the crust starts to brown and the toppings are hot and bubbling. Use caution taking the hot skillet from the oven. Allow to cool for 5 minutes before lifting or sliding the pizza out and serving.

BEST. BURGERS. EVER.

MAKES 4 TO 6 BURGERS ✦ ACTIVE TIME: 30 MINUTES ✦ START TO FINISH: 30 MINUTES

I won't argue that a burger hot off the grill is a delicious thing. It's a staple of American dining. But if you want the Best. Burger. Ever., you won't produce it on the grill. You'll make it in a cast-iron skillet. Period. Why? Because the fat in the meat creates its own sauce, helping to brown and flavor the meat as it cooks. All of this drips off the grill. The cast-iron holds the heat steady and hot, too, turning the surface of the burger the perfect crispy dark brown from side to side. If your mouth is watering now, wait until you make this at home.

1 pound ground beef

Salt and pepper
for seasoning

Hamburger buns
(not too bready)

Slices of cheese
(optional)

Lettuce, tomato,
and onion (optional)

Ketchup, mustard,
pickles, mayonnaise
(optional)

1. Refrigerate the hamburger meat until ready to use.

2. When it's time to make the burgers, first brush your skillet with a thin sheen of oil, and heat it over medium-high heat. Take the meat out of the fridge and form the patties. Don't overhandle the meat, simply take a handful of it (about 3 oz.), and gently form into a patty. Make 3 or 4, depending on how many will fit in the skillet.

3. Put the patties in the skillet and don't touch them. Let them start to cook on the medium-high heat. They'll spatter and sizzle. That's fine. Sprinkle some salt on them, and grind some pepper over them (but not too much). Let them cook on one side for about 3 minutes.

4. When you flip the burgers, if you want cheese on one or all of them, put it on now. The cheese should blanket the meat, not be an afterthought.

5. Leave the burgers to cook on this side just as you did the other side. The skillet takes care of even distribution of the heat. Wait 3 or 4 minutes. Scoop the burger off the skillet with the spatula, slide it onto a bun, top with whatever you like, and dig in. Best. Burgers. Ever.

The kind of meat you use matters. The meat-to-fat ratio should be about 80-20. Most ground beef found in the grocery store is 85-15 or 90-10. If you have to go with one of these, choose the fattier proportion. The best thing to do, though, is ask the meat department to grind the meat for you. You want a chuck cut with a good amount of fat in it. The fat should show up as almost chunky in the meat, not pulverized into the grind to look like pale red mush. Trust me on this one.

STEAK FRITES

SERVES 2 ✦ **ACTIVE TIME: 30 MINUTES** ✦ **START TO FINISH: 2 HOURS**

A hot, juicy steak… yummy. A mound of hot, crispy French fries… fabulous! Now combine them, and you'll understand why the French have this dish on the menu of nearly every bistro in the country. And you can create them both in your skillet.

For the Fries

1 pound Yukon gold potatoes, peeled, washed, and cut into thin strips

3 cups peanut oil (Although increasingly difficult to find, peanut is the best oil to fry in. If you can't find it, vegetable oil is a suitable substitute.)

Salt and pepper to taste

For the Steak

2 small steaks (best is sirloin, rib eye, or shell), about 1 inch thick

3 tablespoons unsalted butter

Salt and pepper to taste

Fresh parsley for garnish

1. Preheat the oven to 200 degrees.

2. Prepare everything ahead of time so you can cook the steaks immediately after the fries. If you wait too long, the fries will get soft. Line a baking sheet with paper towels (for the fries when they're cooked). Put the steaks on a plate in the refrigerator (keep them cold until ready for to go in the pan). Make sure your potato strips are clean and dry.

3. Put the oil in the skillet and add the potatoes. Bring the oil to a boil over medium-high heat (careful of splattering). As the oil gets hotter, the potatoes will get limp and just start to brown (about 15 minutes). At this point, start turning them with tongs to get all sides crispy and browned. Cook another 5 minutes or so.

4. Transfer the fries to the baking sheet and sprinkle with salt. Put in the oven to stay warm, covering with additional paper towels so they stay crisp.

5. Drain the fat from the skillet into a heat-proof glass container (like a measuring cup). Put the skillet back on the burner and add the butter. Take the steaks out of the fridge. When the butter is hot but not smoking, put the steaks in the skillet. Sear them over the high heat for a minute per side, then reduce the heat to medium. Sprinkle with salt and pepper and turn them every few minutes. They're cooked in about 8 minutes (so that they're somewhat rare and juicy inside).

6. Transfer to plates, and pile the French fries next to them. Garnish with parsley. Voila!

BEEF BRISKET

SERVES 6 TO 8 ✦ ACTIVE TIME: 30 MINUTES ✦ START TO FINISH: 9 HOURS

Brisket is the name of the cut of meat from a cow that's taken from the breast. It is a tough piece of meat that needs a long, slow cooking time—but it's worth it, because the slow cooking tenderizes the meat and brings out the flavor. A little prep time, and the meat can cook in the skillet in the oven for a solid 8 hours, leaving you free to do other things.

8-pound brisket, with a layer of fat on it or with marbling of fat

1 teaspoon vegetable oil

Salt and pepper

1. Preheat the oven to 250 degrees.

2. Heat a large cast-iron skillet over medium-high heat. When it's hot, add the vegetable oil, and then put the brisket in fat side down so it starts to cook. Sear the meat on both sides, about 3 minutes a side, and season with salt and pepper.

3. Put the skillet in the oven with the brisket facing fat side up. Cook for 8 hours, checking on it every few hours to be sure it isn't drying out, but this is unlikely.

4. Cook until the meat is very tender, falling apart with a fork.

Some serious BBQ competitions feature brisket, and different chefs have different "secret ingredients" to transform this cut. Some use barbeque rubs with everything from cayenne to cumin to special peppers. Some start the heat high and then lower it. If you want a flavored brisket, explore putting a rub together. You'll need to add it as you would the salt and pepper in this recipe. But I prefer to serve the basic brisket with different barbeque sauces on the side.

CHICKEN FAJITAS

SERVES 6 TO 8 ✦ ACTIVE TIME: 30 MINUTES ✦ START TO FINISH: 5 HOURS

The trick is to bring this dish to the table while the meat and veggies are still sizzling. You'll want to be sure you have all the sides prepped ahead of time so you can go straight from stove to table with this. You'll want tortillas, guacamole, salsa, jalapenos, sliced black olives, and sour cream.

For the Chicken

½ cup orange juice

1 lime, squeezed (about 3 tablespoons juice)

4 cloves garlic, minced

1 jalapeno pepper, ribs and seeds removed, diced

2 tablespoons fresh cilantro, chopped

1 teaspoon cumin

1 teaspoon dried oregano

Salt and pepper

3 tablespoons olive oil

3 to 4 boneless, skinless chicken breasts, cut into strips

For the Vegetables

2 tablespoons olive oil

1 red onion, thinly sliced

1 red bell pepper, ribs and seeds removed, thinly sliced

1 green bell pepper, ribs and seeds removed, thinly sliced

1 yellow bell pepper, ribs and seeds removed, thinly sliced

2 jalapeno peppers or serrano chiles, ribs and seeds removed, sliced thin

3 cloves garlic, minced

¼ cup fresh-squeezed lime juice

½ cup fresh cilantro, chopped

Salt and pepper to taste

You can use the same ingredients to make steak fajitas, but substitute 1 pound of flank steak for the chicken, and marinate it in the mix overnight. Don't slice the steak until it has been cooked.

1. In a bowl, combine orange juice, lime juice, garlic, jalapeno, cilantro, cumin, oregano, and salt and pepper. When thoroughly combined, add the olive oil. Put the chicken pieces in the mix, stir, cover with plastic wrap and refrigerate for about 4 hours.

2. About an hour before you want to eat, get the sides prepared so you'll have them on hand when the dish is sizzling.

3. Heat the skillet over medium-high heat. Remove the chicken from the marinade with a slotted spoon and put it in the skillet, stirring and turning the pieces so they brown on all sides. Cook thoroughly, about 8 to 10 minutes. Transfer the cooked chicken to a platter and cover loosely with foil to keep warm.

4. Reduce the heat to medium, add the oil, and then add the onion, peppers, jalapeno, and garlic. Cook, stirring, for 3 to 5 minutes until vegetables soften. Add the lime juice and cilantro and cook for a few minutes more. Season with salt and pepper.

5. While vegetables are still sizzling, push them to one side of the pan and put the chicken on the other side. Serve immediately.

CRAB CAKES

**MAKES 6 CAKES ✦ ACTIVE TIME: 60 MINUTES ✦
START TO FINISH: 90 MINUTES**

With these cakes, if you want great flavor, you have to go for top-quality crab meat. This is the kind that's in the refrigerated section of your store's fish department. Don't buy crab meat that's canned like tuna. It has neither the flavor nor the consistency needed for these cakes.

**1 pound lump
crab meat**

¼ cup onion, minced

½ cup breadcrumbs

**1 teaspoon
Worcestershire sauce**

**1 teaspoon Old
Bay seasoning**

**1 teaspoon dried
parsley flakes**

**1 tablespoon
mayonnaise**

1 tablespoon milk

**1 large egg,
lightly beaten**

**Salt and freshly
ground pepper
to taste**

**¼ cup oil (preferably
peanut, but olive
is fine)**

Lemon wedges

1. In a large bowl combine crab meat, onion, breadcrumbs, Worcestershire sauce, Old Bay seasoning, parsley flakes, and mayonnaise. Mix the milk into the egg and add to the crab mix, blending gently but thoroughly. Season with salt and pepper. If mix seems dry, add some more mayonnaise.

2. Heat the skillet over medium-high heat. Add the oil. It should be about ¼-inch deep. When oil is hot, add 3 or 4 individual heaping spoons full of crab mix to the skillet, pressing down on the tops of each to form a patty (cake). Brown the cakes on each side for about 3 minutes. Try to turn the cakes over just once. If you're worried about them being cooked through, put a lid on the skillet for a minute or so after they've browned on each side.

3. Transfer the cakes to a plate and cover with foil to keep them warm while you cook the next batch. Serve on a platter with lemon wedges.

Crabs in the Chesapeake Bay area of Maryland are served with Old Bay seasoning. The Old Bay Seasoning mix you purchase in a store is a proprietary blend, so the proportions aren't known for sure, but it's a combination of celery salt, paprika, cayenne, cloves, ginger, allspice, mustard, cinnamon, and more. The package says it's good on crabs, shrimp, and chicken—and those who love it agree. There's even a potato chip flavored with Old Bay.

PORK CHOPS WITH CIDER AND APPLES

SERVES 4 ✦ ACTIVE TIME: 3 HOURS ✦ START TO FINISH: 4 HOURS

Pork is the perfect accompaniment to apples, and the lovely glaze created in the skillet adds another element of deliciousness. I prefer chops with the bones in, but boneless chops are fine, too.

4 pork chops, about ½-inch thick, bone-in or boneless

Salt and pepper

2 tablespoons olive oil

1 onion, diced

3 cloves garlic, minced

3 tablespoons flour

1½ cups apple cider

2 tablespoons fresh parsley, chopped

1 teaspoon dried sage

1 teaspoon fresh thyme

2 tablespoons butter

3 large apples, cored, peeled and sliced

1 tablespoon sugar

½ teaspoon cinnamon (if desired)

1. Preheat the oven to 350 degrees.

2. Season the chops with salt and pepper. Heat the skillet over medium-high heat. Add the olive oil and coat the bottom. Add the chops and sear on both sides, about 3 minutes a side. Transfer to a plate.

3. Add the onion and garlic to the skillet and stir, cooking, until onion is translucent, about 3 minutes.

4. Reduce the heat to low and stir in the flour, cooking for about a minute. Slowly add the cider, using a whisk to combine it with the flour and onions. Whisk constantly as you slowly add and incorporate the cider. When it is all mixed, increase the heat to medium, stir occasionally, and bring to a boil, simmering at a boil for a few minutes.

5. Stir in the parsley, sage, and thyme, then add the chops. When the sauce returns to a boil, remove it, cover it, and put the skillet in the oven. Bake for 1½ hours until the chops are very tender.

6. When there is about 20 minutes of cooking time left for the chops, prepare the apples.

7. Heat another skillet over medium-high heat and add the butter. When it is melted, add the apple slices. Reduce the heat to low and cook, stirring occasionally, until they start to soften. Sprinkle them with the sugar and cinnamon (if desired), and continue to cook until soft.

8. Serve the chops with the apples, drizzling some of the sauce from the skillet over both.

SUPER-EASY SPARERIBS

SERVES 2 TO 4   ACTIVE TIME: 2 HOURS   START TO FINISH: 2 HOURS

Oven roasting in a skillet renders tender ribs with no hassle. Make these on a cold winter night, and you can pretend you're at a summertime picnic.

2 pounds pork spareribs

Salt and pepper for seasoning

Juice from ½ lemon

1 to 2 cups barbeque sauce

Preheat the oven to 350 degrees.

Wash and dry the ribs, cutting into sections that will fit in the skillet. Season both sides with salt and pepper.

Put the ribs in the skillet, sprinkle with fresh-squeezed lemon juice, and put the skillet in the oven. Bake for about 90 minutes, turning halfway through cooking time.

For the second half of the cooking time, brush with barbeque sauce, if desired, and turn again for the last 15 minutes, putting barbeque sauce on the other side of the ribs. Serve immediately.

BEEF STROGANOFF

SERVES 4 TO 6 ✦ ACTIVE TIME: 40 MINUTES ✦ START TO FINISH: 90 MINUTES

The history of this dish in my house is that it was a favorite of my family's when I was growing up, so I made it for mine as they were growing up. I'm happy to say that they've liked mine as much as I liked my mother's. But the dish itself is Russian (Stroganov), made with pieces of beef served in a rich sauce that includes sour cream (Smetana). It purportedly became popular in the mid-1800s.

1 tablespoon olive oil

1 pound beef stew pieces, cut into strips

1 small onion, minced

2 cloves garlic, pressed

½ cup mushroom caps, sliced

1½ cups beef broth

¼ cup dry sherry

1 tablespoon Worcestershire sauce

¼ cup flour

½ cup sour cream

Salt and pepper to taste

1. Heat olive oil in the skillet over medium-high heat. Add the beef slices so they fit in the skillet (or work in batches). Fry them in the skillet turning so that all sides get browned, about 3 minutes. Transfer the beef pieces to a plate and cover with foil to keep warm.

2. Add a bit more oil if necessary, and sauté the onion, garlic, and mushrooms until soft, about 5 minutes. In the skillet, add the beef broth, sherry, and Worcestershire sauce. Bring to a boil, scraping the browned bits of meat and vegetables off the bottom of the pan. Put the flour in a bowl and add some of the heated sauce, using a whisk to form a paste. Add a bit more sauce to the bowl, and when the sauce is incorporated with the flour, stir all of it into the skillet and mix. Continue to cook until the sauce thickens somewhat.

3. Reduce the heat and add the sour cream. Add the meat pieces back to the skillet. When everything is hot, serve. Season with salt and pepper.

This dish must be served over egg noodles. Nothing else will do. Chop some fresh parsley to use as a garnish if desired, and have some bread available to lap up the extra sauce.

FRIED CHICKEN

SERVES 4 ✦ ACTIVE TIME: 60 MINUTES ✦ START TO FINISH: 90 MINUTES

If you want the texture and flavor of chicken fried in oil without the mess of the oil, try this recipe. The corn flakes are essential!

3 chicken legs (drums and thighs together, cut to make 3 drumsticks and 3 thighs)

¼ cup flour

Salt and pepper

1 cup milk

1 tablespoon white vinegar

2 eggs, lightly beaten

1½ cups corn flakes, finely crushed

½ cup plain breadcrumbs

1 teaspoon paprika

1 cup vegetable oil

1. Preheat the oven to 400 degrees. Place the skillet in the oven to get it hot.

2. Rinse and dry the chicken pieces.

3. In a shallow bowl or cake pan, whisk together the flour with some salt and pepper. In the measuring cup of milk, add the vinegar and let the combination sit for 10 minutes (to create buttermilk). When ready, mix the milk in a bowl with the beaten eggs. In another large bowl, combine the corn flakes, breadcrumbs, paprika, and 2 tablespoons of the vegetable oil.

4. Coat the chicken pieces one at a time by dipping each in the flour, then the milk mixture, then the crumb mixture, being sure to coat all sides. When coated, put the pieces on a plate, cover with plastic wrap, and refrigerate for about 15 minutes.

5. Remembering how hot it's going to be (wear oven mitts!), take the skillet out of the oven and put the oil in it. Heat it on low until hot. Add the cold chicken pieces and turn in the hot oil so both sides are coated with oil.

6. Put the skillet back in the oven and bake for about 30 minutes, turning the pieces after 15 minutes. The chicken is done when the juices run clear when pierced with a knife. Serve immediately.

SIMPLE SKILLET SALMON

Start with super-fresh fish, and keep it simple—butter, lemon, salt, and pepper—and you can create a succulent dish that is ready in no time.

3 to 4 pounds salmon filets

2 tablespoons unsalted butter, cut in pieces, softened

1 lemon

Salt and pepper

1 tablespoon oil

1. Rinse the filets with cold water to ensure that any scales or bones are removed. Dry them in paper towels. Rub soft butter on both sides of the filets, squeeze lemon over them, and season with salt and pepper.

2. Heat the skillet over medium-high heat and add the tablespoon of olive oil. Add the filets, flesh side down. Cook on one side for about 3 minutes, then flip them and cook only 2 minutes on the other side. Remove the pan from the heat and let the fish rest in it for a minute before serving. The skin should peel right off.

There are different cuts of salmon steaks and filets. The steaks are cut from the meat around the backbone, and they contain that bone in the middle. Filets are cut from the flesh that extends from the head to the tail of the fish. For this recipe, use filets.

SAUSAGE AND PEPPERS

SERVES 4 TO 6 ✦ ACTIVE TIME: 40 MINUTES ✦ START TO FINISH: 60 MINUTES

This combination is so delicious. It includes onions, as well. Sauté everything until it is crispy and caramelized, and serve the sausages in large sandwich rolls.

4 tablespoons
olive oil

1 pound sweet
Italian sausages

4 cloves garlic,
sliced thin

2 green bell peppers,
ribs and seeds
removed, sliced thin

1 red bell pepper, ribs
and seeds removed,
sliced thin

2 hot peppers like
Italian, Poblano,
or Hungarian hot
wax (or 1 jalapeno),
ribs and seeds
removed, sliced thin

1 large onion,
sliced thin

Salt and pepper
to taste

1. Preheat oven to 350 degrees.

2. Heat the skillet over medium-high heat. Add 1 tablespoon of olive oil. Sauté the sausages in the oil until golden brown on all sides—about 3 minutes a side. Transfer the sausages to a plate.

3. Add the additional oil, and add the garlic, peppers, and onion. Cook, stirring, while vegetables soften, about 5 to 6 minutes. Return the sausages to the skillet.

4. Put the skillet in the oven and bake for about 15 minutes, until sausages are cooked through and vegetables are tender and slightly crunchy on the outsides. Season with salt and pepper. Serve with long sandwich buns, and hot pepper flakes if desired.

SIDE DISHES

In my opinion, this is where a lot of the magic happens in cooking—especially with a cast-iron skillet—because there are so many ingredients to play with. Vegetables, starches, grains, spices, sauces—you'll see what I mean when you thumb through this chapter. Deliciousness happens over and over, and with simple ingredients that are easy to find, affordable, and satisfying for the whole family.

STUFFED TOMATOES

MAKES 6 SERVINGS ✦ ACTIVE TIME: 1 HOUR ✦ START TO FINISH: 2 HOURS

These are great filled with a stuffing with meat in it or without. The sidebar adapts the recipe for a meatless version.

6 ripe large tomatoes

1 pound sausage, casings removed

1 onion, diced

4 cloves garlic, minced

2 teaspoons red pepper flakes (optional)

8 white mushrooms, stems removed, diced

½ green bell pepper, seeds removed, diced

2 cups plain breadcrumbs

2 tablespoons dried sage

1 cup grated Parmesan cheese

Salt and pepper to taste

1. Preheat the oven to 375 degrees.

2. Core the tomatoes, and using a small paring knife or a serrated grapefruit spoon, scoop out the insides. Once hollowed, sprinkle salt on the insides and turn upside down on a plate covered with a paper towel to absorb the water. Let sit for about 30 minutes

3. Heat the skillet over medium-high heat and cook the sausage, breaking it up as it cooks. Cook until there is no pink showing in the meat. When cooked, transfer the sausage to a large bowl using a slotted spoon. In the sausage fat, cook the onion and garlic until translucent, about 4 minutes. Add the mushrooms and peppers and continue to cook, over medium heat, stirring, until vegetables soften, about 10 minutes. Add red pepper flakes if desired.

4. Add the mushroom mixture to the sausage and combine. Then add the breadcrumbs, sage, and Parmesan. Season to taste with salt and pepper.

5. Wipe down the skillet and brush with olive oil. Position the tomatoes in the skillet bottoms down. Start filling the tomatoes gently, dividing the filling between them. Cover the tomatoes with aluminum foil and put the skillet in the oven. Bake for about 30 minutes, remove the foil, and continue baking for another 10 to 15 minutes until cooked through. Serve hot.

Meatless Stuffed Tomatoes: If you want to make this without sausage, simply omit that ingredient. Double the amount of mushrooms, and after sautéing the mushrooms and peppers, drain the excess liquid. You can also add toasted walnut pieces for additional flavor and fiber.

RATATOUILLE

SERVES 4   ACTIVE TIME: 40 MINUTES   START TO FINISH: 2 HOURS

There are variations on this dish—some insist that zucchini is a necessary ingredient—but I like it with just eggplant, peppers, and tomatoes—and garlic, of course.

⅓ cup olive oil

6 cloves garlic, minced

1 medium eggplant, cut into bite-sized cubes

2 peppers, seeded and diced

4 tomatoes, seeded and chopped

Salt and pepper to taste

Heat half the olive oil in the skillet over medium-high heat. Add the garlic and eggplant and cook, stirring, until pieces are coated with oil and just starting to cook, about 2 minutes. Reduce the heat slightly and add the peppers and additional oil, stirring to combine. With the heat on medium, cover the skillet and let cook, stirring every few minutes to be sure vegetables aren't sticking to the bottom of the pan. If the mix seems to dry, add a little more olive oil. As the eggplant softens, the dish will regain moisture.

After about 15 minutes, when the eggplant and peppers are nearly soft, add the tomatoes and stir to combine. With the lid off, continue to cook the ratatouille, stirring occasionally, until the eggplant and peppers are soft and the tomatoes are wilted. Remove the skillet from the heat, season with salt and pepper, and allow to sit for at least 1 hour. Reheat and eat.

If you want to make this with zucchini, choose a small one, and cut it into thin half-moon pieces. Add the zucchini with the peppers.

POTATO PANCAKES

MAKES 6 TO 8 SERVINGS ✦ ACTIVE TIME: 60 MINUTES ✦
START TO FINISH: 90 MINUTES

The way to make the best-tasting potato pancakes is to get as much liquid out of the grated potatoes and onions as possible. This is a bit time-consuming, but it's worth it! You can also prepare the potato-onion mixture a day or two earlier and keep the mix in an airtight container in the refrigerator.

6 large russet potatoes, washed and peeled

1 large onion

3 eggs, beaten

¼ to ½ cup matzoh meal

Salt and freshly ground pepper

1 cup canola or vegetable oil

1. Using a hand grater or a food processor with a shredding attachment, grate the potatoes onto a large baking dish, and then transfer to a colander in the sink.

2. Grate the onion or use a knife to process into a very fine dice. Put the grated onion into a bowl.

3. Squeeze as much liquid out of the potatoes as possible. Take half of the grated potatoes, mix them with the onions, and process the mixture in a food processor or blender to create a rough puree. Don't over-blend or chop, as the mix will get too starchy.

4. Put the puree in a separate colander so that it can drain. Let both colanders drain for another 20 to 30 minutes. Push down on both to release more liquid and squeeze them again before continuing with the recipe.

5. Combine the two batches into a large bowl, and add the eggs and matzoh meal. Stir to thoroughly combine. Season with salt and pepper.

6. Heat the skillet over medium-high heat and add the oil. Be careful making the pancakes, as the oil can splatter. Take spoonfuls of the potato mix and place them in the oil. Cook for about 3 minutes a side. The pancakes should be golden brown on the outside and cooked through on the inside. You may need to adjust the temperature of the oil to get the right cooking temperature, especially if you have more than three in the skillet at one time.

7. When cooked, transfer with a slotted spoon to a plate lined with paper towels. Keep warm until ready to eat. Season with additional salt and pepper.

Variations

- Serve with chunky unsweetened applesauce and a small dollop of sour cream.

- Serve as you would French fries—with salt and vinegar, with ketchup, with gravy, or with salsa.

- For a nontraditional taco, top potato pancakes with chili and cheese.

ROASTED ROOT VEGETABLES

MAKES 4 TO 6 SERVINGS ✦ ACTIVE TIME: 20 MINUTES ✦ START TO FINISH: 60 MINUTES

If you find yourself home from the farmer's market on a fall morning with bunches of root vegetables that looked so good at the market but are now baffling you as a cook, this recipe will save you.

2 small parsnips, trimmed and scrubbed clean

1 turnip, trimmed and scrubbed clean

4 small beets, trimmed and scrubbed clean

4 medium carrots, trimmed and scrubbed clean

½ onion, cut into slices

1 small bulb fennel, trimmed and cut into slivers

¼ cup olive oil

Salt and pepper to taste

2 teaspoons dried rosemary, crumbled

1. Preheat the oven to 400 degrees.

2. Cut the cleaned vegetables in half or quarters to form bite-sized pieces.

3. In a large bowl, combine all cut vegetables and pour the olive oil over them. Season with salt and pepper and toss to coat.

4. Put the vegetables in the skillet and sprinkle the rosemary over everything.

5. Put the skillet in the oven and bake for about 40 minutes, turning the vegetables over after the first 20 minutes. Serve warm.

Variation

Substitute herbes de Provence for the rosemary. This is a French blend of rosemary, fennel, basil, thyme, marjoram, basil, tarragon, and lavender—all the goodness of a Provencal herb garden.

ONE-POT MAC-AND-CHEESE

MAKES 6 TO 8 SERVINGS ✦ ACTIVE TIME: 30 MINUTES ✦ START TO FINISH: 60 MINUTES

There's nothing like homemade macaroni and cheese, but it can get as messy to make as it is to eat when you have to use several pots and pans to make and serve it. Here comes your cast-iron skillet to the rescue!

1 pound elbow macaroni (uncooked)

1 tablespoon salt

3 tablespoons butter, room temperature

3½ tablespoons flour

1½ cups milk, room temperature or slightly warmed

¼ cup sour cream

¾ pound sharp white cheddar, grated

¼ pound Gruyére cheese, grated

Salt and pepper to taste

Dash of cayenne pepper

1. Preheat the oven to 425 degrees.

2. Put the macaroni in the skillet and add cold water so that it reaches ¼ inch below the top. Stir in the salt, turn the heat on to high, and cook the macaroni as the water boils for about 10 minutes. Test a piece after about 7 minutes. The pasta should be al dente—nearly cooked through but still a bit chewy. When it is cooked like this, drain it in a colander over a large mixing bowl so the water is retained.

3. Put your skillet back on the stove over medium heat, and add the butter. When it's melted, stir in the flour with a wooden spoon if possible, stirring constantly so no lumps form. When it is starting to bubble, start adding the milk, whisking constantly as you add it slowly. Add about a ½ cup at a time, being sure to whisk it thoroughly before continuing. When all the milk is stirred in, let the sauce simmer over low heat for about 10 minutes until thickened.

4. On low to medium heat, stir in the sour cream. When the mix is warm again, stir in the cheeses, stirring gently as they melt. Season with the salt, pepper, and cayenne.

5. Finally, add the macaroni gently into the cheese sauce. If it seems too thick, add some of the macaroni water. The consistency should be like a thick stew. When the noodles are hot, transfer the skillet to the oven.

6. Bake in the oven for about 15 minutes, then take a peek. The dish should be bubbling and the cheese on the top starting to brown. This takes somewhere between 15 and 25 minutes. Be careful not to let it burn. Let the macaroni cool slightly before serving.

Variations

Macaroni and cheese is a dish that's great fun to personalize. There are all sorts of ways you can change it up a bit. Try using different amounts of different cheeses (but always those that melt well, which are typically hard cheeses or aged cheeses); add bacon bits; add chopped (seeded) tomatoes; add chopped green onions; add jalapeno peppers; sprinkle breadcrumbs on top for a crunchy layer; or try using different pasta shapes like mini penne, orecchiette, or even pinwheels.

SKILLET EGGPLANT PARM

SERVES 4 ✦ ACTIVE TIME: 20 MINUTES ✦ START TO FINISH: 60 MINUTES

Gooey goodness straight from the skillet, rich with garlic, fresh mozzarella, and Parmesan cheese—and the eggplant isn't fried, so it's not too heavy.

1 large eggplant

Salt for sprinkling on eggplant

2 tablespoons olive oil

1 cup Italian seasoned breadcrumbs

2 tablespoons grated Parmesan cheese

1 egg, beaten

Prepared spaghetti sauce (no sugar or meat added)

2 cloves garlic, pressed through a garlic press

8 oz. mozzarella cheese, shredded

1. Preheat the oven to 350 degrees.

2. Trim the top and bottom off the eggplant and slice into ¼-inch slices. Put the slices on paper towels in a single layer, sprinkle salt over them, and leave them for about 15 minutes. Turn the slices over, salt this side, and let sit for another 15 minutes.

3. Rinse the salt from all the pieces and dry with clean paper towels.

4. Drizzle oil over a baking sheet in preparation for the eggplant.

5. In a shallow bowl, combine the breadcrumbs and Parmesan cheese. Put the beaten egg in another shallow bowl. Dip the slices of eggplant in egg, then breadcrumbs, coating both sides. Put them on the baking sheet.

6. Bake in the oven for about 10 minutes, turn them over, and bake another 10 minutes. Remove the sheet from the oven.

7. Put a layer of spaghetti sauce in the cast-iron skillet and stir in the pressed garlic. Lay the eggplant slices in the sauce, layering to fit. Top with the shredded mozzarella.

8. Put the skillet in the oven and bake for about 30 minutes, until the sauce is bubbling and the cheese is golden. Allow to cool for about 10 minutes, then serve with extra sauce if desired.

HOME-STYLE BAKED BEANS

MAKES 6 TO 8 SERVINGS ✦ ACTIVE TIME: 30 MINUTES ✦ START TO FINISH: 1 ½ TO 2 HOURS

I still have the picture in my head of cowboys cooking in a cast-iron skillet over an open fire while their horses hang out behind them. What are they eating? In my mind, it's baked beans with bacon, which seems quintessentially "skillet cooking" to me. So here's a recipe in honor of my vision.

6 strips thick-cut bacon, divided in half

½ onion, diced

½ cup diced bell pepper (ribs and seeds removed)

1 teaspoon salt

2 (15.5-oz.) cans pinto beans, rinsed and drained

1 cup barbecue sauce (not too sweet!)

1 teaspoon Dijon mustard

2 tablespoons dark brown sugar

Fresh ground pepper

1. Preheat the oven to 325 degrees.

2. Heat the skillet over medium heat and cook half the bacon pieces. Cook until it's just soft, about 8 minutes. Transfer to a plate lined with paper towels to drain.

3. In the fat, add the remaining pieces of bacon, turn up the heat, and cook, flipping often, until pieces are browned. Reduce the heat to medium. Add the onion and pepper and cook, stirring occasionally, until the vegetables soften, another 8 minutes or so.

4. Add the salt, beans, barbecue sauce, mustard, and brown sugar. Stir, season with additional salt and a generous grind of fresh pepper, and leave on the stove until the liquid just starts to simmer.

5. Lay the partially cooked pieces of bacon on top and transfer the skillet to the oven.

6. Bake for 1 hour and take a look. The bacon should be crisp and browned, and the beans should be thick. This can go for another 15 to 30 minutes more if the consistency isn't right. Just be careful not to overcook them, in which case the beans will start to dry out. An hour and 15 to 20 minutes is about right.

7. Remove from the oven and allow to cool slightly before serving, preferably in bowls around a fire!

Baked beans are delicious and filling on their own, but they are the perfect accompaniment to grilled sausages, hot dogs, hamburgers, pork chops, or barbecued chicken. Their thickness is also complemented by coleslaw or a big green salad. Cornbread (page 98) makes the meal.

DESSERTS

As you may have already discovered with recipes in the other chapters of this book, the cast-iron skillet is remarkably versatile, doing its best "work" going from stovetop to oven, it seems, and being able to render something cooked to crunchy perfection on the outside while retaining a moist center. It might be desserts where this quality is best put to use. Did you know your cast-iron skillet is a pie plate? And a cookie sheet (ok, a small one, but still!)? And a cake pan? Best of all, it is a pan in which you can caramelize butter and sugar and sauté bananas, pears, and apples and other fruits to perfection.

APPLE PIE

SERVES 6 TO 8 ✦ ACTIVE TIME: 60 MINUTES ✦ START TO FINISH: 2 HOURS

Impress your friends! Impress your family! Impress yourself—you won't believe how easy this is and how delicious the result!

1 crust recipe for
a double crust
(see page 94 or 96)

6 Granny Smith
apples, peeled, cored,
and sliced

1 teaspoon
ground cinnamon

¾ cup sugar

1 teaspoon fresh
squeezed lemon juice

1 tablespoon butter

1 tablespoon light
brown sugar

1 egg white

1. Preheat the oven to 350 degrees.

2. In a large bowl, toss apples with cinnamon, sugar,
   and lemon juice.

3. Put the skillet over medium heat and melt the butter in it.
   Add the brown sugar and cook, stirring constantly, until sugar
   is dissolved, 1 or 2 minutes. Carefully remove pan from heat.

4. Place 1 of the piecrusts over the sugar mixture. Fill with the
   apple/spice mix, and place the other crust over the apples,
   crimping the edges together.

5. Brush the top crust with the egg white. Cut 4 or 5 slits
   in the middle.

6. Put the skillet in the oven and bake for about 60 minutes
   until golden brown and bubbly. Cover the outermost
   edge with aluminum foil in the last 10 minutes of baking
   to prevent it from burning.

7. Allow to cool before serving. Serve with whipped cream
   or ice cream.

You can flavor whipped cream with liqueur for an especially yummy topping. Beat heavy or whipping cream until soft peaks form. Add about ¼ cup sugar and continue beating until stiff peaks form. Gently beat in ¼ cup liqueur, such as apple brandy or Cointreau. Serve immediately or cover with plastic wrap and refrigerate until ready to serve.

STRAWBERRY RHUBARB PIE

SERVES 6 TO 8 ✦ ACTIVE TIME: 45 MINUTES ✦ START TO FINISH: 2 HOURS

In the spring, Rhubarb is one of the earliest things to reappear in the gardens of those of us who live in the Northeast, and so it is celebrated. Rhubarb is naturally tart, which is why it works so well with strawberries, which, when fresh, are bursting with sweetness.

1 crust recipe for a double crust (see page 94 or 96)

4-5 stalks rhubarb, cleaned and cut into 1-inch pieces (use about 1½ pounds frozen rhubarb, thawed, if fresh isn't available)

1 quart fresh strawberries, washed and tops trimmed, and sliced in half or quarters (use ½ pound frozen strawberries, thawed, if fresh aren't available)

¾ cup sugar

⅓ cup flour

1 tablespoon butter

1 egg white

1. Preheat the oven to 375 degrees.

2. In a large bowl, toss rhubarb and strawberries with sugar and flour.

3. Put the skillet over medium heat and melt the butter in it. Carefully remove pan from heat.

4. Place 1 of the piecrusts in the skillet. Fill with rhubarb/strawberry mix, and place the other crust over the fruit, crimping the edges together.

5. Brush the top crust with the egg white. Cut 4 or 5 slits in the middle.

6. Put the skillet in the oven and bake for about 45 to 55 minutes until golden brown and bubbly. Cover the outermost edge with aluminum foil in the last 10 minutes of baking to prevent it from burning.

7. Allow to cool before serving. Serve with whipped cream.

PUMPKIN PIE

SERVES 6 TO 8 ✦ ACTIVE TIME: 30 MINUTES ✦ START TO FINISH: 90 MINUTES

With the butter/sugar combo underneath the pie shell, the result is a crisp, sweet crust topped with an earthy, smooth pumpkin filling. It really works.

1 crust recipe for a single crust (see page 94 or 96)

1 (15-oz.) can pumpkin puree

1 (12-oz.) can evaporated milk

2 eggs, lightly beaten

½ cup sugar

½ teaspoon salt

1 teaspoon cinnamon

¼ teaspoon ground ginger

¼ teaspoon ground nutmeg

1 tablespoon butter

1 tablespoon light brown sugar

1. Preheat the oven to 400 degrees.

2. In a large bowl, combine the pumpkin puree, evaporated milk, eggs, sugar, salt, cinnamon, ginger, and nutmeg. Stir to combine thoroughly.

3. Put the skillet over medium heat and melt the butter in it. Add the brown sugar and cook, stirring constantly, until sugar is dissolved, 1 or 2 minutes. Carefully remove pan from heat.

4. Place the piecrust over the sugar mixture. Fill with the pumpkin mix.

5. Put the skillet in the oven and bake for 15 minutes, then reduce the heat to 325 degrees and bake an additional 30 to 45 minutes until the filling is firm and a toothpick inserted in the middle comes out clean. Don't overcook.

6. Allow to cool before serving. Serve with fresh whipped cream.

CARROT CAKE

SERVES 8 ✦ ACTIVE TIME: 20 MINUTES ✦ START TO FINISH: 60 MINUTES

This recipe makes a delicious and moist carrot cake. It's especially tasty when frosted with an easy-to-make cream cheese frosting (see sidebar).

8 tablespoons
(1 stick) butter

1 cup julienned
carrots, chopped fine

1½ cups golden raisins

1 (15.25-oz.) box
of carrot cake mix

¾ cup water

⅔ cup vegetable oil

6 oz. unsweetened
applesauce

4 eggs

1. Preheat the oven to 350 degrees.

2. In the skillet, melt the butter over medium heat. When it's melted, add the carrots and raisins. Simmer them in the butter over low to medium heat until the butter is bubbling.

3. In a large bowl, combine the cake mix, water, oil, applesauce, and eggs. Stir to combine.

4. When the butter in the skillet is bubbling, turn off the heat and pour the batter over the carrot/raisin mix.

5. Bake 35 to 40 minutes until browned on the top and sides and a toothpick inserted in the middle comes out clean.

6. Allow to cool for about 10 minutes. The skillet will still be hot. Put a large serving plate on the counter and, working quickly and deliberately, flip the skillet so the cake is inverted onto the plate. Allow to cool before frosting.

EASY CREAM CHEESE FROSTING

This makes enough to frost the skillet cake, which is a single layer.

6 oz. cream cheese,
at room temperature

4 tablespoons
unsalted butter,
at room temperature

1¼ cups
confectioner's sugar

½ teaspoon vanilla extract

In a large bowl, combine all ingredients. With an electric mixer, beat on medium until well combined and smooth. Spread over cooled cake.

SKILLET S'MORES

If you planned a cookout and the weather didn't cooperate, trust your cast-iron skillet to save the evening when you gather the kids and others around to share this campfire treat.

1 (16.5-oz.) bag semi-sweet chocolate chips

16 marshmallows

Cut in half Graham crackers

1. Preheat the oven to 450 degrees.

2. Put the chocolate chips in the skillet and top with the cut marshmallows, clean side facing up.

3. Bake in the oven until marshmallows brown on top, about 5 minutes.

4. Serve with graham crackers for scooping and a side of ghost stories.

Americans eat more marshmallows than any other country, maybe because the modern manufacturing of them was established in the Chicago area in the early 1950s by Duomak. The confection we enjoy today is far removed from its original source—the root of the Althaea officinalis, a marshland flower. It was the ancient Egyptians who first extracted its sweet sap.

Today's commercially available marshmallows are made with spun sugar, water, and gelatin. More and more confectionery retailers are offering homemade marshmallows, and it's not difficult to make them yourself. They are yummy!

THE BEST SKILLET BROWNIES

SERVES 6 TO 8 ✦ ACTIVE TIME: 40 MINUTES ✦ START TO FINISH: 90 MINUTES

If you're serious about chocolate brownies, you'll love this recipe. When shopping for the ingredients, remember that the better quality the chocolate, the better the taste and texture of the brownie. You may be tempted to eat the whole thing by yourself, and that wouldn't be good.

10 tablespoons unsalted butter

8 oz. semi-sweet chocolate, coarsely chopped

1 cup sugar

3 eggs at room temperature

1 teaspoon vanilla extract

½ cup + 2 tablespoons all-purpose flour

2 tablespoons unsweetened cocoa powder

¼ teaspoon salt

1 cup semi-sweet chocolate chips

1. Preheat the oven to 350 degrees.

2. In a microwave-safe bowl, melt the butter and chocolate pieces together, cooking in 15-second increments and stirring after each increment. The butter and chocolate should be just melted together and smooth.

3. In a large bowl, whisk the sugar in with the eggs. Add the vanilla and stir to combine. Working in batches, start mixing the melted chocolate into the sugar/egg mixture, stirring vigorously to combine after each addition. In a small bowl, mix the flour, cocoa powder, and salt. Gently fold the dry ingredients into the chocolate mix. Next, fold in the chocolate chips.

4. Over medium heat, melt 1 tablespoon butter in the skillet. When melted, pour in the batter. Bake for about 30 minutes or until a toothpick inserted in the center comes out with a few moist crumbs. It may need a couple more minutes, but be careful not to over-bake this or you'll lose the great gooiness. When it's ready, remove from the oven and allow to cool about 10 minutes.

5. Dig right in, or scoop into bowls and serve with your favorite ice cream.

Variation

Enhance the flavor further and add a ½ teaspoon of peppermint extract and 1½ cups York Peppermint Patty pieces to the batter.

BAKED APPLES

MAKES 4 SERVINGS ✦ ACTIVE TIME: 30 MINUTES ✦
START TO FINISH: 50 MINUTES

These are easy to make and are delicious served warm or at room temperature the next day. Of course, they're best with a side of vanilla ice cream or even maple Greek yogurt.

4 firm apples

2 tablespoons butter

½ cup water

Maple syrup

1. Preheat the oven to 350 degrees.

2. Peel the apples, leaving a ring of peel on the bottom where the apple will stand in the skillet. Get as much of the core out without cutting the apple in half.

3. Heat the skillet over medium-high. Add the butter and let it melt. Place the apples bottom-down in the skillet. Add the water from the center so that it distributes evenly around the apples. Drizzle the tops of the apples with maple syrup.

4. Put the skillet in the oven and cook for about 20 minutes, or until apples are soft. Drizzle with additional maple syrup if desired.

Variation

Use apple cider instead of water to make a nice apple-butter sauce, which you can simmer down after the apples are cooked to make a concentrated sauce.

GIANT CHOCOLATE CHIP COOKIE

MAKES 1 LARGE COOKIE   ACTIVE TIME: 20 MINUTES
START TO FINISH: 45 MINUTES

Yes, your cast-iron skillet is also a great baking sheet—just smaller, and with sides.
So why not cook a giant cookie in it? Here's how.

1 cup butter, softened

½ cup white sugar

1 cup brown sugar

2 eggs

2 teaspoons
vanilla extract

1 teaspoon
baking soda

2 teaspoons hot water

½ teaspoon salt

2½ cups flour

2 cups semisweet
chocolate chips

Preheat oven to 375 degrees. Heat the skillet in the oven while making the batter.

In a large bowl, cream together the butter and sugars. Add the eggs one at a time, being sure to combine thoroughly before proceeding. Stir in the vanilla.

Dissolve the baking soda in the hot water and add to the batter along with the salt. Stir in the flour and chocolate chips.

Remove the skillet from the oven and put the batter in it, smoothing the top with a spatula.

Put the skillet in the oven and cook until golden, about 15 minutes. Serve with ice cream.

If you like nuts in your chocolate chip cookies, you can add them here. Mix in ½ cup walnut or almond pieces when adding the flour and chocolate chips.

CHOCOLATE CAKE

SERVES 4 ✦ ACTIVE TIME: 20 MINUTES ✦ START TO FINISH: 60 MINUTES

This is another winner that you'll want to serve again and again either plain or with a topping of your choice. Who doesn't appreciate chocolate cake?

6 tablespoons butter, cut in pieces

1 cup sugar

2 eggs

½ teaspoon vanilla extract

1 cup flour

1 teaspoon baking powder

2 tablespoons unsweetened cocoa powder

½ cup milk

1. Preheat oven to 350 degrees.

2. In a large bowl, cream the butter and sugar together until light. Add the eggs one at a time, combining thoroughly after each addition. Stir in the vanilla extract.

3. In a small bowl, combine the flour, baking powder, and cocoa powder, and mix the dry ingredients together. Alternately add the flour mix and the milk to the butter-sugar mix until thoroughly combined.

4. Grease the skillet with some butter and add the cake batter.

5. Put in the oven and bake for about 30 to 35 minutes, until the top is golden and the cake springs to the touch and a toothpick inserted in the middle comes out clean. Cool and cut into wedges.

Variations

There are so many ways to top this simple chocolate cake, including whipped cream, frosting, fresh berries, berries and cream, chocolate syrup, ice cream (almost any flavor), or marshmallow fluff.

METRIC CONVERSION CHART

US measurement	Approximate metric liquid measurement	Approximate metric dry measurement
1 teaspoon	5 mL	
1 tablespoon or $1/2$ ounce	15 mL	14 g
1 ounce or $1/8$ cup	30 mL	29 g
$1/4$ cup or 2 ounces	60 mL	57 g
$1/3$ cup	80 mL	
$1/2$ cup or 4 ounces	120 mL	$1/4$ pound/ 113 g
$2/3$ cup	160 mL	
$3/4$ cup or 6 ounces	180 mL	
1 cup or 8 ounces or $1/2$ pint	240 mL	$1/2$ pound/ 227 g
1 $1/2$ cups or 12 ounces	350 mL	
2 cups or 1 pint or 16 ounces	475 mL	1 pound/ 454 g
3 cups or 1 $1/2$ pints	700 mL	
4 cups or 2 pints or 1 quart	950 mL	

ABOUT CIDER MILL PRESS BOOK PUBLISHERS

Good ideas ripen with time. From seed to harvest, Cider Mill Press brings fine reading, information, and entertainment together between the covers of its creatively crafted books. Our Cider Mill bears fruit twice a year, publishing a new crop of titles each spring and fall.

"Where Good Books Are Ready for Press"

Visit us on the Web at
www.cidermillpress.com
or write to us at
PO Box 454
12 Spring St.
Kennebunkport, Maine 04046